# CREATING AUTHENTICITY IN
# STEAM
# EDUCATION

# CREATING AUTHENTICITY IN STEAM EDUCATION

A project-based learning and design thinking approach

## MICHELLE BRADLEY

Published in 2024 by Amba Press, Melbourne, Australia
www.ambapress.com.au

© Michelle Bradley 2024

All rights reserved. No part of this book may be reproduced or transmitted in any form or by any means, electronic or mechanical, including photocopying, recording or by any information storage and retrieval system, without prior permission in writing from the publisher.

Cover design: Tess McCabe
Editor: Andrew Campbell

ISBN: 9781923116450 (pbk)
ISBN: 9781923116443 (ebk)

A catalogue record for this book is available from the National Library of Australia.

# Contents

About the author — vii
Acknowledgements — viii
Introduction — 1

## Part 1: Beginning to understand the pedagogy — 5

*Chapter 1*    Project-based learning — 7
*Chapter 2*    Design thinking — 15
*Chapter 3*    Understanding STEAM — 22
*Chapter 4*    Further pedagogical concepts behind the framework — 25

## Part 2: The Authentic STEAM Framework — 33

*Chapter 5*    What is the Authentic STEAM Framework? — 35
*Chapter 6*    Stimulus and resources — 37
*Chapter 7*    Brainstorm and research — 44
*Chapter 8*    Design and simplify — 51
*Chapter 9*    Prototype and refine — 56
*Chapter 10*    Present and evaluate — 62

## Part 3: Designing authentic examples — 65

*Chapter 11*    Building resources — 67
*Chapter 12*    Authentic examples — 73
*Chapter 13*    Microlearning content — 83

## Part 4: The Simplified STEAM Framework — 91

*Chapter 14*    The Simplified STEAM Framework — 93
*Chapter 15*    The Primary-based STEAM Framework — 105

| Part 5 | Microlearnings and skill development | **121** |
|---|---|---|
| *Chapter 16* | Algorithms, mind maps and structure | 123 |
| *Chapter 17* | Coding | 130 |
| *Chapter 18* | Virtual and augmented reality | 144 |
| *Chapter 19* | General skills | 192 |

## Part 6: Developing authenticity across the curriculum — 211

| *Chapter 20* | Beginning integration of STEAM learning | 213 |
|---|---|---|
| *Chapter 21* | A cross-curricular and extra-curricular approach | 226 |

## Part 7: Authentic assessments — 233

| *Chapter 22* | Creating personalised contracts | 235 |
|---|---|---|
| *Chapter 23* | The theory behind updating how we assess | 239 |

| Conclusion | 249 |
|---|---|
| Bibliography | 250 |

# About the author

I did not become a teacher for the right reasons. My degree (Bachelor of Applied Science, with majors in mathematics and digital technology, and minors in chemistry and physics) could have led me to become either a programmer or a teacher. At that time, I thought I could not see myself programming full-time, so I went into teaching. My father was a primary school principal at that time and did not want either of his daughters to become teachers. Probably not surprisingly, we both did, though my sister works in early childhood while I work with Grades 7 to 12.

While I did not get into it for the right reasons, I quickly came to love it. I started teaching digital technologies before the internet and Google existed, and have worked in education, industry and enrichment programs since then. My areas of expertise are science, technology and mathematics. I also love to paint and create, and this has given me a unique perspective on teaching STEAM and understanding how creativity enhances learning.

I worked for around 10 years as a computer trainer, programmer and documentation expert with a private company in Hobart, Tasmania. This opened my eyes to the gifts of change management and building bespoke systems for clients.

After having my sons, I returned to education in Launceston, Tasmania. I found that my stint in the business world had changed my teaching practices and view of the world considerably. With my new knowledge in creating custom systems, I became more focused on differentiating content and creating more personalised and engaging experiences for students. I also began to develop online content that would allow all students to feel safe and supported in the educational environment. This in turn supported them to achieve to the best of their ability.

The framework used in this book is one that I have perfected over many years and use within my STEAM, digital technology, mathematics and science teaching programs. It also considers the role of artificial intelligence (AI) in creating educational disruption and how it can help to promote and inform STEAM education.

# Acknowledgements

I wish to thank the amazing educators and business colleagues I have worked with in the past. I am so grateful for their ability to open my eyes to different ways of thinking and being. They have shown me new skills and led the way for me to follow in their footsteps. This in turn has allowed me to create programs and systems that help students to thrive with their existing experiences, abilities and understanding.

I often say that being an educator is not what I do, but who I am. It is a wonderful thing to be surrounded by educators who are as passionate about education as I am, and I am grateful for their guidance and support.

This book is dedicated to my family, who support and encourage me always, and from whom I inherited the "how hard could it be?" gene. Their support is constant, unwavering and all-encompassing.

My final thanks go to my three sons, Angus, Jonah and Campbell, who inspire me every day to be better and do better.

*Michelle*

# Introduction

Teaching in the 21st century requires constant pivoting, skill development and adaptation, particularly within digital technology and STEAM education. As digital natives, the students I teach now understand and view the world in vastly different ways compared to students in the early part of my teaching career. They also interact with that world in ways I could never have imagined.

The advent of artificial intelligence (AI) will see a future with not only digital natives, but AI natives. How will we teach them? How will we prepare them for a world in which they need to learn, unlearn, then learn again on repeat? I find the possibilities of these questions exciting and intriguing. However, I also understand that a massive (and seemingly insurmountable at times) learning curve must be negotiated to meet the needs of our students, particularly with this new horizon of artificial intelligence looming.

I truly believe that to teach 21st-century lifelong learners, educators must also become 21st-century lifelong learners. I am hoping that this book is a starting point on your journey of learning.

I have worked in STEAM since the early years of my teaching career, though at that time the focus was more specifically on STEM. While there are similarities between the two, which are discussed in detail in this book, the biggest different is the A – which stands for Art or Artistic. To me, this is the creative component that provides the special glow to the already amazing world of STEM Education.

I believe my industry experience has been essential to my growth as an educator. It has allowed me to view the world quite differently – and my place in it. I love the challenge of stimulating students to try new things and think creatively within the STEAM genre. I know that if students are given the correct guidance and stimuli they can create and innovate in ways that they never could if their self- and world-view were limited.

Educators are passionate and dedicated, but we are also overstretched and – let us be honest – tired. Adding to the mental load we already carry is not the aim of this book. The idea behind this book is to ease the burden by showing a clear path of manageable steps. It has been designed to be dipped into, to help you find your inspiration and beyond everything just keep moving forward. This should be a conversation, not a lecture.

The ideal teaching and learning style is to give students what they need, when they need it, and in the way that they need it. But dealing with so many different needs, backgrounds and skills can be overwhelming. "One size fits all" is just not a viable option, but an approach heading towards personalised learning cannot happen all in one go. This means a lot more initial work, but overall gives a deeper and more satisfying learning experience – for both the students and the educator. The same skill-development methodology is useful for educators as we navigate this new and exciting time in education.

Here are some key suggestions that will help as you begin this journey:

- **Just begin.** Saying "Yes" to something you are not sure of can be frightening, but it can also be invigorating! Sometimes it just takes the courage to begin and learn as you go.
- **Take baby steps.** Microlearnings are incremental learning experiences that will be discussed in a great deal of detail in this book. Microlearnings are smaller pieces of the bigger educational picture and are essential to success in STEAM and design thinking. They are relevant learnings for any given task and help support learning in the moment. They allow students (and educators) to pick up the skills they need, when they need them, in the way they need them.
- **Do not be afraid to admit you do not know.** A huge lesson to learn is that we cannot know everything. Admitting gaps in knowledge to a peer or student can be an empowering experience for both of you. It gives you an opportunity to say, "I'm not sure – let's find out together". This shows the student that it is OK to admit a need for help and provides strategies for gaining knowledge. Developing lifelong learners is a large part of our remit as educators, and this is a step on the right path.
- **If it does not go as well as you hoped, tweak and begin anew.** Sometimes you just need to take a chance on a challenge, and – let's face it – it may not work out how you wanted. That is fine; just take what was good, adjust and move on. Do better next time.

- **Work as part of a team.** Brainstorming and developing with others is a great way to develop your skills, whether in person or online. Working together to build resources can reduce workload, but often results in more authentic tasks. Almulla (2020) discusses the importance of working as part of an educational team, which "allows teachers to share knowledge and skills in a variety of subjects, leading to a transition from expert learner to expert". There is also evidence that when "receiving support from peers, teachers can achieve higher performances" (Walsh & Elmslie, 2005).
- **Work smarter, not harder.** You do not have to be an expert today. Begin with one task, trial it with a class, then develop another. A transformation of the whole program does not have to be completed today. The key is just to begin.
- **Find the fun.** If it is fun for you, the students will enjoy it. Find the joy and fun, which will in turn help to develop creativity in yourself and your students. If you enjoy it, they will too, and finding fun in learning is key to educational success.
- **Develop cross-curriculum strategies.** As you develop skills and programs, try to think outside the box and create challenges that would work across curriculum areas to build deeper meaning for your students.
- **Begin with the end in mind.** As we will see in later chapters, where we delve into the detail, it is important to think about what you hope to achieve before you develop programs. Ask yourself questions like:
    - What skills would you like your students to leave school with?
    - How will you develop these skills in a methodical and incremental way as they pass through different stages of learning?
    - How will you empower students and educators to build on their knowledge and develop their skills and abilities?
    - How can you create intrinsically motivated students?

While these questions will be explored in detail throughout this book, our initial focus should be on the development of "21st Century skills consisting of knowledge construction, real-world problem solving, skilled communication, collaboration, use of information and communication technology for learning, and self-regulation" (Stehle & Peters-Burton, 2019).

The next few chapters will focus on the relevant theories and pedagogies that make up the Authentic STEAM Framework and will help guide you on how to create enriching STEAM experiences within your school.

## STEAMauthenticity.com
### More than just straws and Plasticine

Throughout this book are references to resources and videos. STEAMauthenticity.com has been set up to provide support materials and full versions of challenges, templates and workbooks. Also available to purchase are microlearning videos that will support your professional learning and help to develop your educational practice.

This book is meant to be a resource to dip into, to enjoy, and to build your skills and confidence. My hope is that it provides support and inspiration to begin or continue your STEAM journey.

*Michelle*

# PART 1
# BEGINNING TO UNDERSTAND THE PEDAGOGY

Alice laughed: "There's no use trying," she said; "one can't believe impossible things."

"I daresay you haven't had much practice," said the Queen. "When I was younger, I always did it for half an hour a day. Why, sometimes I've believed as many as six impossible things before breakfast."

– *ALICE IN WONDERLAND* BY LEWIS CARROLL

CHAPTER 1

# Project-based learning

Solving real-world problems quickly and strategically is essential to the preparation of your students for the world they are going to be part of. One pedagogy that is regularly used is project-based learning. Project-based learning is a teaching method that allows students to learn by doing. Instead of dealing in abstract concepts, project-based learning allows students to relate learnt concepts back to the solution of real-life tasks. By following this approach, long-term transfer is a realistic result. Long-term transfer is when a student learns a necessary concept, not just for the short term, but for the long term. It also ensures that students gain deeper long-term understanding of concepts covered and can then relate those concepts to their own life. Basically, it means learning for a lifetime, not just for a test or assignment.

When working within project-based learning, students are presented with open-ended challenges and then use their skills either individually or as teams to complete iterative solutions, working towards an end goal. An open-ended challenge is one that is phrased in such a way that the question will have multiple possible end points, depending on how a student interprets it. It also creates an iterative process, geared towards continuous improvement.

Here is a simple example:

| Change your thinking from | To become |
|---|---|
| Listing bridge types for different situations. | 1. Ask students to design a bridge that would suit different situations.<br>2. Get them to research their design, then build a scale version of the bridge. Specifications could include:<br>• The weight the bridge could hold<br>• How much movement it would withstand (earthquake, weight). |

Project-based learning promotes deeper learning in various ways. These are discussed below.

## 1. Real engagement in meaningful projects

As an adult, it is often difficult to get excited about completing tasks which do not seem to have any real meaning or purpose. The same is true for students. Making meaning is essential for everyone and increases student uptake. Disengaged students often distract others and make learning difficult. Through project-based learning techniques, it is possible to link the learning to real life, and in this way re-engage the disengaged and strengthen the resolve of others. In other words, we are not doing work to answer a test; we are learning so that we can solve this problem.

> Recently a group of my Year 12 students were asked to work out a solution to the problems experienced by parents and other visitors to our school website. My educational approach to that could have been to tell them all the problems and to identify ways that these could have been fixed. They could have then turned that list into an essay or PowerPoint to understand the problem.
>
> Instead, they engaged in a survey, obtained details from various stakeholders, and collected data from the school website. They decided that a chatbot was the best solution across all platforms and set about finding a way to build a prototype. They looked at what might be expected or required of a successful chatbot.
>
> Once a software platform had been decided upon (they used Dialogflow), they built a model and started teaching it the information it needed to succeed.
>
> The best part for me? Listening to the problem-solving, questioning and designing as they worked on the solution and troubleshot without me.
>
> Did I feel redundant? Absolutely not. Because their ability to question and learn outstripped my need to be the bringer of all knowledge.
>
> The end point? They made a presentation to our principal and marketing team about the need for change and what their suggestions were. It was an amazing experience for all. If I had given them the list, it would have been forgotten soon after (probably the day of) the exam. This is something that will shape who they are and their belief in their own abilities for the rest of their lives.

## 2. High-quality work that is understood well rather than restated

We have all taught students who are great at completing tests. They know how to revise, how to test themselves, and how to retain the information – at least for short periods of time. Those students are often applauded and congratulated on their ability to get high marks – as they should be.

But the question always remains: do these students really have a strong understanding of what they are "learning"? Many do, but there must be a way to create meaningful teaching and learning experiences to allow students with different learning styles not only to achieve at a high level but also to show understanding and long-term retention of knowledge.

Project-based learning encourages deeper learning. It motivates learning for a purpose, and solidifies that learning through action, invention and iteration. It isn't just learning for a test but learning for a purpose.

## 3. Answering a driving question and developing student agency

Project-based learning is very effective at developing student agency. Student agency is the development of choice for students either individually or within groups. This choice is developed in project-based learning using driving questions. Driving questions are questions within a task that allow students to have control over how they respond to the task.

The OECD Future of Education and Skills 2030 project discusses how "student agency and learning have a circular relationship. When students are agents in their learning, that is, when they play an active role in deciding what and how they will learn, they tend to show greater motivation to learn and are more likely to define objectives for their learning" (OECD, 2019).

This might be self- or teacher-initiated, but is always open to interpretation by the student. It might result in various outcomes, methods of delivery or approaches. But the responses are always delivered with educators as facilitators, bringing support when required.

Project-based learning is key to the development of student agency because project-based learning tasks are set so that a myriad of viable responses can bring completion – limited only by student imagination and choice.

I like to think I have a good imagination, but when students are encouraged to develop agency, the results are so amazing I am blown away every time. The classroom becomes an exciting and innovative place to exist, and I wouldn't be anywhere else.

## 4. Working as a team

Project-based learning, if used correctly, allows students to develop skills as part of a team – to find where their strengths and weaknesses lie and how those strengths and weaknesses work with others on the team. Resilience, self-expression and project management strategies are just three of the areas in which working as a team allows student development. The concept of teams and how they can be used effectively will be discussed in detail in later chapters.

## 5. Higher-order thinking skills (HOTS)

Higher-order thinking skills are deeper thinking and learning processes than might be expected through traditional educational formats. Some examples of higher-order thinking skills are:

- **Critical thinking.** This is the ability to see different options and opinions and weigh up in a methodical way which suit a particular situation or project. Critical thinking, also known as divergent thinking, "is about applying logic, refining, narrowing down, and evaluating options; in short, analysing and criticizing" (Green, 2021).
- **Metacognition.** This is the ability to think about and understand how you think and break concepts down. Students (and educators) become aware of strengths and weaknesses, focusing on developing skills that enhance the former and build strength in the latter.
- **Application.** Being able to see a process or skill used in one area and see how it is possible to adapt it to another application.

## 6. The development of creativity

This is one of the least understood but most important advantages of project-based learning. Creativity is often misconstrued as being great at painting or drawing. This could not be further from the truth. It is the "ability to come up with unique and valuable solutions for problems" (Green, 2021).

Green goes on further to argue that "creativity is an expression of your imaginative mind, and you can express your creativity in many ways".

In summary, this means that project-based learning gives meaning to learning, through a real-life approach which in turn produces better end results and deeper thinking processes. It helps students develop critical thinking, problem-solving, collaboration and communication skills. The components of project-based learning are given various names, but the basic premise of the process is the same. They include the following:

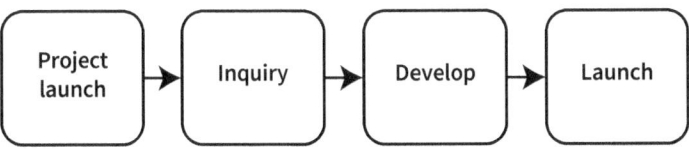

## *Project launch*

This is the first stage of the project-based learning approach. It is also the most important part of the process, as everything flows from this point. It is important to create an effective driving question to get the project started.

Driving questions reach the heart of the project being investigated. They are open-ended, challenging and thought-provoking, and encourage students to research and respond in a way that brings them outside their comfort zones.

By using an effective driving question, students will find natural interest and focus within the question. This in turn will lead to completion of the project launch component. It is essential that driving questions are easily relatable and mappable to the required content. Driving questions must also pique the interest of the desired audience and be framed in such a way as to increase the students' desire to build a response to the content.

An example of a driving question:

> Are we good neighbours? How can we create a better relationship with Asian and Pacific countries?

## *Inquiry*

The inquiry phase of the project-based learning framework relates to two concepts: ideation and inquiry. Simply put, ideation is the process of brainstorming and tangential thinking that allows students to come up with new and engaging ideas. Inquiry then follows on from that starting point.

Inquiry is the process of questioning and exploring these ideas. Problems are explored and tested through this process, and solutions are examined critically.

One part of this process cannot work without the other. The process of ideation and inquiry requires an active role in learning and requires educators to embrace a facilitation role, rather than that of information-bringer.

Educators should provide resources and guidance, but the control of the task returns to and remains with the students. Educators can also provide support in this stage by encouraging students to find appropriate resources to inform their responses, and by encouraging students to assign roles within their teams. Both of these activities will promote focus within the group and help to develop cooperative responses.

The idea is to create many different possible end points and solutions for the task, then challenge and test those possible solutions for the best fit. This is what makes the project-based learning framework effective. Through research, questioning and testing different outcomes, the inquiry phase can help to find the best-fit solution.

A key component of the inquiry phase is exposing your students to many different mentors, resources and stimuli. Green (2021) points out that "the way you see things depends on so many different factors. There is no one correct perception of an issue. Different people will have different perspectives, and all these perspectives are valid".

Embracing and applying these diverse views will ensure that students are more creative in their approaches and will develop critical thinking and problem-solving ability. The development of these skills will aid in their development as 21st-century learners.

> Ideation responses to the "Are we good neighbours?" question could include:
> - Educational and resource-sharing projects
> - Safety around hardware and software dumping
> - Climate change issues
> - Offshore businesses not paying workers well to produce cheaper clothing and products.

## Develop

Develop is the third stage of the project-based learning framework. It is the time where concepts are developed, critiqued and then revised. Once the ideation and inquiry component has been completed, the development process can begin in earnest.

However, the process of inquiry and revision of solutions is not something that finishes within the inquiry section. To develop solutions to driving questions, it is essential to constantly refer to the original question and ensure that, through the iterative process, the final solutions reflect the original project goals. The PBL Toolkit (2023) defines driving questions as "open-ended inquiry that guides students' thinking and learning".

The PBL toolkit goes on to argue that driving questions need to "connect with learning goals, spark discussion or debate, raise additional questions, and endure over time". Driving questions, then, become the anchor and essential element that drives the idea of project-based learning.

By beginning to debate, question and query the provided driving question, it is then possible to begin to design and develop our solutions. Designing a solution to the project goals and developing prototypes will require constant questioning and re-evaluation. There will then need to be a testing and questioning phase that will refine the solution to meet the project goal more effectively.

A further essential component is prototyping. Prototyping is the development of the visual component of the process and will ensure that any issues not yet identified can be ironed out. Testing for compatibility with real-world situations may lead to some further refinement. At this stage it is often useful to ask for outside feedback and content from independent parties or subject matter experts, so that the product can then be further refined.

This stage must focus on constant development, refinement and adjustment to ensure that the original task requirement is met.

> Developing a new business model for working with Asian and Pacific countries might be a response for the "good neighbours" question. It might include:
> - Better working conditions for workers
> - Education for the children of workers
> - Profit-sharing for workers.

## Launch

This is the final phase of the project-based learning framework in which the completion and presentation of the final solution takes place.

After the constant refinement of the develop phase, this phase allows students to use the knowledge and skills gained throughout the project-based learning process. Students must revise their work to ensure that it meets the project requirements.

Once the design of the solution has been completed, students will present their project findings and solution to an audience. This may be peers, their teachers or topic mentors. Feedback can be sought from the audience but should aim to focus on areas of strength and be constructive to help to improve the final product.

On completion of the presentation, students provide feedback on the project. This may be reflection on the project itself, including areas of improvement, or could focus on peer- or self-reflection.

Some key points of focus could be:

- What have you learnt?
- What did you do well?
- What could you do better next time?
- How can what you have learnt be applied to other projects?

### Summary of key points

- Project-based learning focuses on real-world solutions to real-world problems.
- Students will improve higher-order thinking skills (HOTS) and problem-solving ability.
- The project-based learning approach requires the teacher to be the facilitator and the student to take more control of their own learning experience.
- Project-based learning encourages a continual questioning and revising process, with constant reference back to the original task.

CHAPTER 2

# Design thinking

Do you ever have an idea pop into your head and then forget about it, only to find out later that someone has already come up with the same concept and made a lot of money out of it? "Big sky thinking" is a term for looking at problems creatively and then brainstorming solutions.

Do you think about questions such as:

- How would it solve the problem?
- What would it look like?
- What would it need to make it attractive and useful to those that need it?
- How could I make this happen?

These questions are part of "design thinking". This is the process of taking a "big sky" concept into something that is manageable and focused for the group it is created for. The aim of this chapter is to understand the concepts surrounding design thinking, then be able to support students and educators in creating strong ideas and having the confidence and skills to follow these ideas through.

## What makes good design?

Good design can be very subjective – what seems pleasing and useful to one is not necessarily pleasing to all.

There are many components to good design, and several of the key requirements are listed below:

- **Is it fit for purpose?** Does it do what it is meant to do? Good design means that the product meets its intended purpose, and is easy to use and understand.

- **Does it solve a problem or meet a need?** A variation or adjustment or change may make the solution to the problem more suitable and useful.
- **Is it innovative and/or useful?** Innovative and useful design can often meet a need that was not seen before. It can present a solution from another perspective that was not previously clear.
- **Is it user-centred?** Is there a person or group of people that this product or design is perfect for? This will be discussed further below.
- **Is the change meaningful or useful?** Do not change for change's sake. While change is wonderful, there should only be change if it is an improvement on what came before.

This section will focus on defining design thinking and developing an understanding of how it works. It will also look at *why* design thinking is beneficial and why it works so well with STEAM options. The key components of this section are:

- What is design thinking?
- What are the advantages of using design thinking?
- Why does it work so well with STEAM?

## What is design thinking?

Design thinking is a method of creatively solving problems by means of a user-centred focus. It allows individuals or groups to use creativity as a tool to develop more detailed and relevant solutions to design challenges. These challenges can be used in a classroom environment to promote authenticity within teaching and learning.

Many parts of the design thinking framework will seem familiar, as they map directly to project-based learning. It is user-centred and involves constant iterations to move closer to a satisfactory end point that meets the needs of the target customer. These iterations are essential to successful completion of a task or project.

The key difference between design thinking and project-based learning is that the latter is generally an educational tool to encourage students to create solutions that focus on applying knowledge and skills to a real-world project. On the other hand, design thinking is a problem-solving methodology that can be applied in educational and professional contexts. It allows students "to arrive at innovative solutions, developing into autonomous learners who are responsible for their own learning" (Lee, 2018). It also provides students with "the vehicle for inquiry, teaching them how to think, reason, analyse, empathise, and use their natural curiosity to find solutions" (Lee, 2018).

This book will focus on combining the two pedagogies to create the Authentic STEAM Framework.

## Components of design thinking

The concepts of design thinking will be referred to throughout this book. With that in mind, the components are described below to provide a deeper understanding of the overall process.

### *Conduct research*

This involves breaking the question down into components and keywords to ensure that the question is understood. This can be done through asking questions – of a topic specialist and/or mentor or members of your own team.

Research can also be undertaken through internet searches. These need to be focused and easy to lift from the open-ended question. It is also useful to try some tangential thinking – adapting a concept or idea that does not directly relate to the concept to create a new way of approaching the project.

An essential part of the research process is to keep track of any links and references (websites, texts, content from mentors) in case they need to be referred to later. Keeping track of this information will ensure that these references can be annotated or referred to later if necessary.

Use this research to get a deeper understanding of all aspects of the problem, and share this with all members of the group.

The following question might be proposed as a challenge task:

> How can we provide equal accessibility to an active lifestyle?
> The research might start by looking at:
> - What does an "active lifestyle" mean?

- Who might have difficulties maintaining an active lifestyle?
- What are the limitations and concerns of people in these groups?
- Who might already be supporting these groups?
- Where are the gaps in support for these groups?

## *Brainstorm: Understand the process or problem*

There is no such thing as a bad idea – even the craziest options could end up as a great product idea. Talking together and freestyling thoughts does mean that a lot of very strange, tangential thinking may take place. However, the best concepts often come from iterations of these random ideas.

Once the initial free flow of ideas is completed, talking as a group allows ideas to be refined and expanded. At this point, removal of ideas is not necessarily part of this process. Use the time to bounce ideas off one another, research further, then refine.

> With the active lifestyle question, brainstorming might lead to these subsequent questions:
> - How could hearing-impaired or visually impaired people participate in team sports?
> - Could a person in a wheelchair or with other mobility issues participate in martial arts training?
> - Could there be a project that would allow elderly people to participate in an active lifestyle and improve both physical and mental wellbeing?

## *Improve: Highlight and fix issues*

In this component, it is time to narrow down the process and discuss within the group:

- What works well?
- What could work better?
- What are some modifications you could make to improve the product?
- What needs to be thought about further?

> With the active lifestyle question, one subsequent question would be focused on – for example, the question about promoting the physical and mental wellbeing of elderly people.
>
> The discussion might centre around a product or project that might help elderly people. This might be a group within a school that pairs

up younger and older people to play games or where the older person teaches the younger person skills. The rationale behind this might be the overarching question: "What do elderly people need the most to promote their physical and mental wellbeing?" The answer to that might be promoting connections.

## Create prototype: *What the product or project might look like*

Referring to the target customer is an essential part of creating prototypes. It is essential to focus on what their needs and wants are and to seek clarity on the difference between and importance of these two components.

The information from the previous section is essential to success in prototyping. This information will inform decisions made about prototyping.

The fun can begin here.

Creating prototypes of products that can be critiqued and built upon helps to support the final product. A prototype can be an initial drawing or image, and once the final design is created it can be built into a 3D version. If producing a program or process, a mock-up of what that looks like can be created instead.

It is all about the visual. By producing something that the group or client can see or touch, there is a greater chance that it will be understood and accepted.

The important part, though, is the focus on the original target customer and the variations or choices they might like. Variations might come in the form of colour, size, pattern or material, but could also be styles, locations or versions of a plan.

Within this iterative phase, it is essential for students "not to get too attached to their prototypes. [They] may need to make drastic changes to their prototypes or even discard them completely" (Lee, 2018). This is often a difficult concept for students, who tend to get lost in their own brilliance and find it difficult to escape that and return to the iterative process to meet the needs of the task.

Once the variations and prototypes for the target customer have been created, it is time to broaden the appeal to other groups. This means looking at other groups that might like the process or product. Prototypes can then be made for them to broaden the scope of the product.

While it might seem strange to work with target customers, it is an effective tool, allowing focus and progress to be made more quickly.

### *Present: Show to an audience*

Presentation is an essential component of the design thinking process. This does not necessarily mean speaking to large groups. A video "pitch" can be effective, requiring students to speak for 1-2 minutes on:

- The inspiration behind their product or process
- Their target customer and the thinking behind their solution
- Why their solution meets the needs of the target customer
- Details of their solution and prototypes.

Some of the advantages of the design thinking process include:

- Promoting effective teamwork
- Viewing content from different points of view
- Encouraging deeper problem-solving and creativity
- Meeting the requirements of the target customer
- Allowing the expansion of knowledge in a positive and creative way.

The key with the presentation component is to focus on what the person you are presenting needs to hear rather than what you want to tell them – which is also true in our roles as educators!

## How does design thinking work with STEAM?

Design thinking provides structure and scaffolding for educators and students. It creates a step-by-step option that can be completed and then built upon. There are clear end points and instructions for each component. But most importantly, design thinking guides thinking and helps develop creativity.

Developing problem-solving ability and exploring creativity are two of the reasons that STEAM is so wonderful as a teaching and learning tool. They are a perfect match and a great starting point for us to begin the STEAM Authenticity journey.

Henriksen (2017) explains how the combination of design thinking and STEAM "offers guidance and structure to equally engage the analytical and intuitive, the artistic and scientific". She goes on to say that "Creativity, interdisciplinarity, real-world, and problem/project-driven emphases, are central to STEAM, and to design as well".

The beauty of design thinking with STEAM is that it gives educators a framework to work within, while still allowing flexibility and creativity to develop within that framework. The combination is magical to experience.

## Summary of key points

- Design thinking is relevant in educational and business settings, and encourages an innovative, creative and user-centred approach to change.
- Students using design thinking can use these skills to focus on solutions to real-world problems that can be transferred to their current and future lives.
- Design thinking allows freedom, flexibility and excitement to develop in the search for solutions.

CHAPTER 3

# Understanding STEAM

## What is STEAM?

STEAM stands for Science, Technology, Engineering, Art, Mathematics and is a problem- and application-based approach to learning. Through this process, students develop skills in an organic way and develop higher-order thinking skills (HOTS). Basically, it enables educators and students to bring meaning to learning – to educate with real-world problems and solutions and promote student agency and better overall learning outcomes.

> In my time as an educator, bringing meaning to learning has been an essential component of my classroom environment. I remember learning about valence electrons in Grade 8, and doing very well at chemical bonding, Bohr diagrams and so on.
>
> What I don't remember is developing an explanation and understanding of the reason valence electrons exist, what they are, and how they affect chemical bonding, which should have been the beginning of my learning. It may have been taught (I may have been talking), but in the years between Grade 8 and first-year university chemistry, that did not enter my consciousness as a conceptual understanding. It was only when I was asked the question by a student that I came up with a simple answer.
>
> It is now an example of a small way that meaning is brought to learning, and students' experience and understanding are so much deeper as a result.

## STEM vs STEAM

In many ways STEM and STEAM are the same thing, but they differ in one very specific way: STEM education focuses more on the specific learning within science, technology, engineering and mathematics, while STEAM adds an overarching layer of creativity that helps students to relate more effectively to content and to extend higher-order thinking skills.

The "A" in STEAM scares a lot of science, technology and mathematics educators, mostly because art is not a traditional component in these areas. However, the artistic component can be the added flavour or "gloss" that brings the project together. The art component is primarily a focus on creativity and the visual representation of learning.

## Advantages of STEAM

STEAM allows us to think creatively, to problem-solve and consolidate learning. Historically, education has focused on the delivery of content and written assessment tasks that show how well the information has been learnt.

While this is not always true for digital technology as a separate subject, science and mathematics will often hold to traditional teaching and learning formats.

STEAM can be used in several ways: as an information-seeking tool or as a consolidation tool. Either of these will enhance the teaching and learning experience.

STEAM learning is also able to create spaces where students can experiment, feel safe in their ideas and motivations, and discuss subjects that interest them. It allows space where no idea is too "out there" to be analysed and discussed.

## How do project-based learning and design thinking work with STEAM?

Project-based learning provides the stimulus, project research, analysis and questioning, while design thinking helps develop the creativity and problem-solving ability. This begs the question: how can they work together with STEAM?

Using design thinking and project-based learning allows students to become enmeshed in detailed projects that "pique their interest and are more relevant to their lives" (Hölzle & Rhinow, 2019). The continuous struggle to maintain motivation and concentration is reduced significantly when students feel that what they are doing has meaning.

Ananda et al. (2023) state that "a Design Thinking approach used in STEAM learning allows students to do more than merely comprehend the material and produce goods; instead, they can recognise, reflect on, and concentrate on the implementation stage of their creations".

The key phrase in this is "their creations". Students are not a vessel to be filled. They come to us with their own ideas, understandings and experiences. Being in a situation where those elements are not only validated, but encouraged and celebrated, creates a space in which they can begin to trust their own voice and develop a belief in their own value.

In an ever-changing world, the importance of STEAM, project-based learning, and design thinking cannot be underestimated. Students in this quicksilver age need to be able to adapt quickly to new situations, assess quickly what is needed, and pivot in multiple directions at once.

It is our job to get them there, and the skills they will develop using these pedagogies are a great start when doing so.

> When asked if I can solve a problem, I always start with "Yes". This is not because I know everything under the sun. It is because I have learnt to believe in my ability to work anything out and find the most efficient and effective solution. This self-belief (and its associated strategies) is a key element of the design thinking, project-based learning approach. These skills are my primary focus when developing STEAM programs, and the results produced by these programs continue to inform and ignite my teaching practice.

## Summary of key points

- STEAM allows students to develop their understanding in creative and innovative ways.
- The combination of project-based learning and design thinking with STEAM allows the development of tasks that will pique students' interests and enmesh them in their own learning.
- Using these various factors allows students to develop the skills that they will need to be effective and adaptable in their future lives.

CHAPTER 4

# Further pedagogical concepts behind the framework

Over time, several key concepts and pedagogical frameworks have become essential as part of a successful 21st-century approach to digital technology education. These concepts and their relevance are explained in detail below.

## Computational thinking

Many educators understand the importance of coding as part of a 21st-century learning experience, but there is often little understanding of the reason for that importance. Coding can be presented in many forms, using many different software programs, but does not always require the use of computers. Computational thinking is directly related to the development of coding skills.

Computational thinking is often described as a set of problem-solving methods that allow the development of solutions using the processes that a computer would use to solve the problem. ISTE (2021) describes it as "formulating problems in a way that enables us to use a computer and other tools to help solve them".

The key 21st-century skill required for coding is the ability to break large tasks down into smaller tasks that can be followed in a logical order. This is the definition of computational thinking. There is an understanding among educators that there is a need for the development of computational thinking and other 21st-century skills. However, there is a significant gap in their knowledge about how to build these skills in an effective way. Tasks and challenges are often completed in an ad hoc way, with little understanding of the need to build and develop skills in a distinct order.

This is not the fault of the educators, who lack resources in this area and receive inadequate support. This is often due to a lack of understanding as to how these skills can be developed effectively or, perhaps more importantly, how these skill development tasks can be integrated into existing learning experiences without adding to the already busy workload of teachers.

Computational thinking can be broken down into four key areas, which are all equally important:

- Decomposition
- Algorithm
- Pattern recognition
- Abstraction.

Definitions and examples are shown in the table below:

| Decomposition | Algorithm | Pattern recognition | Abstraction |
|---|---|---|---|
| Decomposition is the act of breaking down larger problems into smaller manageable problems | Creating a step-by-step process that is in a specific order of completion | The ability to look at and analyse data to see patterns and simplifications | The ability to streamline a problem to find the simplest way to complete the task |
| *Example:* | *Example:* | *Example:* | *Example:* |
| *Planning a holiday in which you visit multiple cities and need to work out what to do in each city regarding travel, accommodation, etc.* | *Instructions to build a house, where the order of the tasks is essential, e.g. you can't put on the roof before the foundation is done* | *Analysing fingerprints or creating facial-recognition software* | *Finding the formula for the circumference of a circle by comparing the radius to the circumference* |

Each of these components is equally important to the development of computational thinking skills needed for 21st-century learners. Computational thinking helps to develop adults that are equipped for an ever-changing environment – in both their personal and work lives. As shown here, despite the name, it is not always necessary to develop computational thinking using computers. Using a STEAM approach is the ideal way to develop computational thinking through challenges and iterations of task solutions.

Computational thinking creates humans who can look at a problem or situation, analyse what is going on, then find multiple strategies that could support a solution. It can be as simple as starting a conversation with "Let's think this through and see if we can work it out".

## Critical thinking

The world for our students is a constant bombardment of information – some factual, some not, with shades of grey in between. With all that information available, how do they determine what is useful, relevant and important? It is fundamental for our students to be able to look at any given situation, research accurately, then make determinations on what the best solution is. The idea of critical thinking builds on the computational thinking process discussed previously.

Students need to be able to make decisions based on what is in front of them and determine a path based on that information. Heard et al. (2020) identify some of the key skills of strong critical thinkers as the ability to:

- Identify gaps in knowledge
- Discriminate and evaluate information
- Identify patterns and make connections.

Well-defined STEAM challenges are designed specifically to extend children and develop deeper thinking and problem-solving. These challenges will then focus on building the critical thinking skills discussed above.

Artificial intelligence has been around for decades, but ChatGPT has thrown us in the deep end of information overload – for both educators and learners. Students often seem to think that whatever is presented to them from Google, ChatGPT and similar products is gospel. But information gained from AI sources needs to be filtered and processed. It is essential to ensure that students are critically analysing the information presented to them from these sources, which means that it is also essential to double down on the development of critical thinking skills.

If managed in a detailed and thorough way, STEAM and the Authentic STEAM Framework are effective ways to help the process of working out which information can be relied upon and which cannot. Being able to use critical thinking to observe, identify and critically analyse bias and the "truth" of content is an essential skill that our students (and their educators) need to embrace fully.

Another essential component of critical thinking that can be developed through Authentic STEAM education is analysing options for solutions within a certain problem. Creating and critically analysing differing solutions – essentially presenting their argument – forces students to justify their analysis and then work towards narrowing down the options until they reach a final product solution.

This ability to deeply and effectively criticise and analyse a problem to find a solution is not an innate one. By being presented with increasingly difficult problem-solving tasks, with decreasing scaffolding on each task over a sustained period, students will be able to critically analyse concepts, tasks and programs to the point where it becomes a natural part of their educational process.

## Creative thinking

Thinking outside the box, or "tangential thinking", refers to the ability to imagine creatively what could be. Doing what was always done can only get you so far. As a result, creative thinking as a concept is essential to STEAM education and the Authentic STEAM Framework.

Creativity is something that many adults believe they do not have now but did exhibit as a child. The reason for this can be very simple. Rather than worrying about their ability to be creative, children simply believe they can. In other words, they are prepared to be wrong. Somehow, as we get older, this self-belief is eroded, which leads to insecurity about ability. Sir Ken Robinson argued that "if you are not prepared to be wrong you will never come up with anything original" (Robinson, 2006). He goes on further to say that children are educated out of their creative capacities.

Creativity as a form of bravery is often underrated. This does not mean you are going to create the next Mona Lisa (well maybe you will). To think outside the bounds of what you already know is liberating and can bring about exceptional solutions to problems.

Creative thinking requires you to:
- Analyse existing situations
- Define who the target customer for the situation might be

- Be open-minded and think tangentially of a solution or solutions to the problem
- Be able to organise your thoughts into sections that will flow smoothly
- Present that information in a way that shows your consideration and understanding of the issue.

By embracing the concepts of creative thinking, we can enhance learning to the point where both students and educators can get excited about what has been created. It enhances ownership and pride. They will not always get it right, but often by getting it wrong and following that thinking to a different solution, the outcome is far better than they could have imagined. So, embrace the crazy, and see where it leads you.

As a science, digital technology and mathematics educator, the linear nature of these subjects can often make creative thinking seem daunting. But by starting small, and most importantly by encouraging your students to evolve their ideas freely, you will start to see the power of creative thinking.

Ultimately, we want to have students so excited about their learning that they cannot wait to begin, and creative thinking is a very definite and achievable path in that direction.

## Web 3.0

There is no doubt that the internet has changed not only how the world functions, but also how education functions. The exponential changes that have taken place have been directly related to the growth of content available online and speed of access. The details of these increments are shown in the table below, based on information provided in Lal & Lal (2011):

| Web versions | Definitions and what they mean (or have meant) for education |
|---|---|
| Web 1.0 | Web 1.0 was the time of dial-up internet connections and was very much used as a one-way transfer of information. Information was viewed, searched for, and downloaded, but there was no fluid interaction. |
| Web 2.0 | As the internet sped up and was more readily available, Web 2.0 came into play. It provided a two-way flow of ideas and information, for both teachers and educators. This came in the form of blogs, podcasts, wikis and so on. Web 2.0 provided a more dynamic experience, with hardware and software that was more interactive and able to be manipulated and managed by people who were not computer scientists, creating a richer tapestry of educational experiences. |

| Web versions | Definitions and what they mean (or have meant) for education |
|---|---|
| Web 3.0 | Lal & Lal (2011) define Web 3.0 as "a series of combined applications. The core software technology of Web 3.0 is artificial intelligence, which can intelligently learn and understand semantics. Therefore, the application of Web 3.0 technology enables the Internet to be more personalised, accurate and intelligent". |

The three main areas that Web 3.0 will excel in are discussed by Lal & Lal (2011) and summarised below:

1. **Web with intelligence.** This means that educators and students will be able to seamlessly benefit from artificial intelligence in such a way as to enhance learning and data analytics without having to understand the programming behind it. Data analytics is the method of converting raw data to useful insights that can be used, in the case of education, to target teaching and learning more effectively and efficiently.
2. **Personalised approach.** Web 3.0 allows for a more personalised approach to individual learning experiences. Lal & Lal (2011) describe this as "different activities such as information processing, search, formation of personalised portal on the web. Semantic Web would be the core technology for Personalisation in Web 3.0". "Semantic Web" refers to the way that information can now be sourced from many different environments and put together in such a way that both humans (and machines) can understand and interpret it.
3. **Virtualisation.** Due to the massive improvement in graphics, 3D modelling and internet speed, virtualisation is now going to be much more readily available to educators. It refers to the ability to create and work within 3D virtual spaces, to create new and exciting areas for educational experiences to evolve in.

This is such an amazing time to be involved in education, and it is wonderful to be able to use Web 3.0 skills and experiences to develop focused, data-led and accessible learning for our students.

> I still remember my time as a teacher (and student) before the internet. *Encyclopedia Britannica* was one of our main sources for assignments, and card catalogues were a thing (if you know, you know). I often say to my students that I am older than Google. They think for a minute and then ask,

"So how did you find out stuff?" It is a foreign concept to them, and to be honest, I now wonder how we got things done.

A new era is now coming where students will ask, "How did you survive before AI [Artificial Intelligence]?" and I am sure a time will come when we will be unsure of how we coped without it.

Some may see that as something to fear. For me, it is something exciting and wondrous – a magical path waiting to be explored.

The key with the internet, and now with artificial intelligence, is not just to use it, but to use it well – to find the authentic approach that enhances educational practice and makes everything clear. The alternative is to use it to make noise, and work harder not smarter, and that is not a path I am willing to travel down.

## Pedagogy 3.0

As technology has exploded, educators have reacted to the changes and advancements by taking matters into their own hands in an ad hoc manner. There has been a "reactionary approach to advancements in technology with little planning within or standardisation of pedagogical constructs" (Allison and Kendrick, 2015). As we move forward, it will be possible to focus on incorporating new changes within the internet (called Web 3.0) into our pedagogical structures and models. Allison and Kendrick (2015) propose that "Web 3.0 promises to alleviate the concerns associated with the data explosion currently underway by making the Internet more machine friendly".

Basically, Web 2.0 created a massive amount of data via wikis, blogs, and social media platforms. This was all unorganised data. Web 3.0 focuses on "organising" that data into manageable formats. This is where artificial intelligence or big data technologies come into play, as they allow data to be used more effectively.

Pedagogy 3.0 is a critical educational pedagogy for current and future teaching practices. It is often linked with the term "edutainment". This term relates to the use of software, film, television and so on to attract students and enhance learning with an educational context. An example might be an online game that aims to teach the concepts of natural selection and survival of the fittest through gamification.

The prime focus of Pedagogy 3.0 is the effective use of digital technology to promote accessibility and various approaches within our teaching and learning environments. A key component of Pedagogy 3.0 is the change from instructor-led focus to a student-centred educational experience.

STEAM creates an ideal environment for this pedagogy to thrive. Within this framework, it is possible to teach using many different approaches, including:

- **Synchronous** – used at the same time, i.e. teacher-led
- **Asynchronous** – from another time, i.e. recorded and online components
- **Online learning** – fully computer-led
- **Face-to-face learning** – fully teacher-led
- **Hybrid** – a combination of teaching and computer-led.

Ultimately, the focus is on the provision of teaching that the student needs, in the way that they need it, and at the time that they need it. This requires a significant level of understanding and preparation, which can be sustained with support and resources. In the next section, we will explain how this can be achieved, while continuing to provide resources that will help with this.

# PART 2
# THE AUTHENTIC STEAM FRAMEWORK

"Millions saw the apple fall, but only Newton asked WHY?"

– BERNARD BARUCH

# Defining the Authentic STEAM Framework

The Authentic STEAM Framework is a combination of both design thinking and project-based learning, but also borrows elements from all the other pedagogies discussed in the previous section. The basic framework is shown below. This framework will then be broken down into manageable sections to show the best way for it to be used.

CHAPTER 5

# What is the Authentic STEAM Framework?

When I speak to educators about their experiences, the common thread in these conversations is not a lack of passion for their role. Educators want to do more and be more. They want to create effective educational experiences for their students. The issues are mostly time constraints and limited access to skill-building and resource-building opportunities. There are also concerns about where to start, and whether what they do will be correct once they have started.

This is particularly true with STEAM education, and the development of Authentic STEAM programs.

This book and the framework within it have been specifically created to provide schools with support while developing their STEAM programs. Often, while educators begin with the best intentions, there is no overarching approach or continuous building of skills. Staff need time for professional learning, and then time to implement what they have learnt. This leads to confusion about priorities, and issues about where to begin. There can be a definite feeling of not having a clear pathway to success.

The prime focus of Authentic STEAM is to ensure the development of genuine and relevant learning that allows students to:

- Develop their problem-solving ability
- Focus on their creativity
- Approach questioning to allow for a wide range of responses, and encourage deeper STEAM learning
- Understand the fundamentals of effective project-based learning and how to apply those fundamentals
- Encourage teamwork, participation and student agency.
- Promote skills in design thinking.

Overall, the development of STEAM skills will encourage students to question, evaluate and create. It will also allow students to develop an understanding of their skills, and start to believe in the value of their own voice.

With this book and the accompanying resources, you will be able to:
- Understand how to use project-based learning effectively
- Develop skills surrounding design thinking
- Transform this understanding of learning experiences for your students using the Authentic STEAM Framework provided.

## A comparison summary of the Authentic STEAM Framework

| Project-based learning | Design thinking | Authentic STEAM Framework |
|---|---|---|
| Project launch | Define the problem | Stimulus and resources |
| Inquiry | Conduct research | Brainstorm and research |
| Develop | Brainstorm | Design and simplify |
|  | Improve |  |
|  | Create prototype | Prototype and refine |
| Present | Present | Present and evaluate |

The overall aim is to use STEAM to build authentic educational experiences. This means that there is always educational context and a focus on the development of thinking processes among our students.

*It is more than just straws and Plasticine.*

CHAPTER 6

# Stimulus and resources

This is the first component of the Authentic STEAM Framework. As we begin, it is essential to define the problem. This requires both a *stimulus* and *open-ended question* to be provided as a starting point. This concept will be discussed in greater detail in **Part 3: Designing authentic examples**.

Alongside the stimulus, a mentor or subject expert is useful when getting students to define the problem. This person can be a teacher or a subject expert. They can be recorded, online live, or face-to-face. Having an expert involved increases the feeling among students that what they are striving for within the challenge is a real issue, and one worth participating in.

Using stimuli and open-ended questions as a starting point is essential to this process. Once ideas have been generated, research can take place that will clarify any content required or issues surrounding the problem.

This is also the component that deals with any constraints and requirements for the project. Constraints are limits that are placed on the project. These may involve price, timeframe or abilities and are essential to consider before planning solutions. Requirements focus on what are the essential components in providing solutions.

> An example of a design thinking challenge might be: How can we provide equal accessibility to an active lifestyle?

This section will describe in detail the components and process of the Authentic STEAM Framework and give guidance and examples for a hands-on approach. The program has been designed to be dipped into easily and will enable educators to explain concepts to their students effectively.

The framework has been broken down into manageable and logical portions. This will have the added benefit of enhancing the teaching and learning experience once all the components are combined to make a whole.

There are three main components that are included in this first section:
- The question
- The stimulus
- The research.

Each of these components is important to the initial understanding and development of ideas. The process of using these components is explained in the sections below.

## The question

The question is essential to the success of the project. Adequate time must be spent on the development of something that is open-ended and stimulating, allowing students to develop creative solutions.

The best way to showcase this process is to show a recent classroom example.

To promote the relationship between our local farming community and our school, the following question was posed:

> How do we work with Tasmanian quality produce to create a unique and innovative product?

> In this classroom task, students within the five groups were given a choice of local produce: eggs, berries, mushrooms, organic beef, and organic pork. Provided for them was basic information about the businesses:
> - Business name
> - Website and social media presence
> - What the business currently produces.
>
> This information gave a basic understanding of the business that could then be built upon to gain deeper learning. In this case the focus was on a business, but in a different case – for example, creating earthquake-proof structures – the basic details might be where and why earthquakes occur.

By creating an open-ended challenge with the possibility of multiple end points, students will be able to respond to the stimulus uniquely. This promotes creativity and sparks ownership of the challenge. Student responses to open-ended real-life problems consistently show end results that are well above expectations.

Effective questioning is an educational tool that promotes the focus on *How?* and *Why?* rather than *What?* Using this approach encourages deeper thinking and learning. Schwartz et al. (2016) extend this idea further, stating that "question driven learning increases curiosity, purpose, attention and well-connected memories" and that "curiosity keeps a student focused on important content and deepens students' sense of purpose. It affords the opportunity to increase attention to targeted ideas".

Effective questioning means that students are challenged and extended to a deeper level than they might be otherwise. Tofade et al. (2013) recommend that students "generate questions to aid in their exploration or understanding of a subject matter". This can be a helpful component of the development process.

The key to effective questioning can be broken down into the following components:

- Is the question framed in such a way that it will spark interest and curiosity in the intended audience?
- Does the question allow for a multitude of interpretations?
- Are there keywords within the question that will create opportunities for the beginnings of our research process?
- Will it promote healthy risk-taking?

  The question shown above is an example of this effective questioning. Breaking it down:
  - The focus is on local produce and uses the term "unique".
  - The local aspect of using the produce and working with local producers is stimulating and sparks interest.
  - The keywords of "Tasmanian quality produce" and "unique and innovative" give a spark for research.
  - Healthy risk-taking will be promoted because even though it is out of the students' comfort zone to do something like this, it is not so far out of their wheelhouse that they will not take a chance.

An essential part of this process is the role of the facilitator. To facilitate effectively means to give guidance when needed but not to steer students in the direction of your own thoughts and ideas. The role of a good facilitator is to stand back and allow the magic to happen, but step in when needed. If students ask for advice or answers, be supportive, but always put the questioning back onto them – for example, "How do you think you could find that out?" or "What would be a good starting point for research into that?"

> In my early years as an educator, I would often pre-empt what I felt were good solutions to the stimulus or insert myself unnecessarily in the thinking process. While my intentions were good, the end results were not always the best. It did not take me long to realise that by encouraging students' ideas rather than promoting my own, the students came up with solutions that were far more creative and innovative than anything I could have thought up myself.

## The stimulus

The stimulus is the next component that needs to be referred to. While the stimulus is important, it does not have to be an exact model of what the question is asking. Once again, your role as the facilitator is to stimulate and help the development of ideas, not to direct students in the direction you think they should be heading.

The stimulus can be in any form: a subject or business expert, a quote, an image, a news article, a song, a sculpture, a cartoon, a video, or something in any other format that is relevant to the problem. If using a video, it is best to keep it under four minutes, as concentration can be lost, and the message will lose its impact. When using a video, encourage students to watch fully, then return and write down key points for later reference.

General stimuli are useful, particularly as students begin this process. These general stimuli encourage students to think about what they are trying to achieve, and how they can engage others in the process and product. Some examples of these are detailed below.

### Start with the why

Simon Sinek is an author and inspirational speaker who has coined the term "Start with why". In this video, he focuses on the idea that "people don't follow what you do, they follow why you do it": https://www.youtube.com/watch?v=u4ZoJKF_VuA

How is this relevant to open-ended challenges? By using the lens of "Why are we creating this?" we can create something that is relevant, engaging, and captures people's attention. This will be featured more in the brainstorming section, as it is an important concept in many different challenges.

**Making change fun**

Another stimulus I use regularly is The Fun Theory (https://www.thefuntheory.com/), which focuses on the idea that people will make changes if we make it interesting and entertaining for them rather than tedious. This is a great general stimulus to encourage people to make changes in how they do things.

**Great design**

Below is a resource that is used as a starting point for creating great design. Students will have experienced it but would not necessarily understand what great design might look like. This resource will give a simple view into the world of design. Hopefully, it will be a springboard for helping students to understand how to create their own creative and imaginative designs. https://www.youtube.com/watch?v=qp3jHWyPW-E

## *Making stimuli fun*

This is so important. People do not like change and will often need a reason to do so. Part of gaining engagement in this type of task is to make the stimuli fun (or sometimes a little bit weird and crazy!). When asking students to create a safety device for bikes or motorbikes, the set stimulus was a creation (I am still not sure if it was serious or not) of a helmet covered in a wig. The stimulus (https://www.youtube.com/watch?v=KNcLX_hkxR0) allowed them to think way outside the box and be creative by embracing the crazy.

Anything that begins with humour is going to help engage students in learning. Why should learning (and teaching) be serious? The short answer is it doesn't have to be.

# Examples of the stimulus design process

Coming up with the ideas in the first place can often be difficult. Instagram reels, advertisements and diagrams can all play a part in the development of an "idea seed" into a question. A key conceptual understanding is that the stimulus may only be tangentially connected to the final question. The link is up to you to decide.

Some examples of the thought process surrounding stimuli and challenges that have worked well in the past are shown below. Concepts will be taken through idea seed, to concept, to question.

## Example 1: Green technology

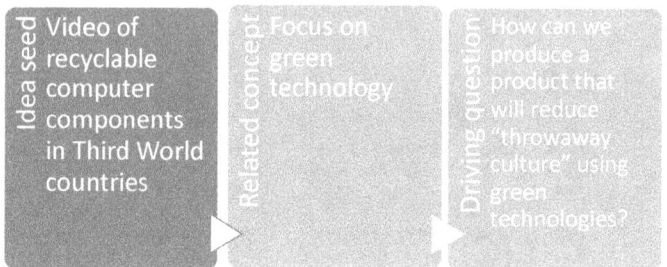

**Idea seed:** Video of recyclable computer components in Third World countries

**Related concept:** Focus on green technology

**Driving question:** How can we produce a product that will reduce "throwaway culture" using green technologies?

**Related resources**
- An excellent video on the true meaning of sustainability: Leyla Acaroglu: "Paper beats plastic? How to rethink environmental folklore." https://www.youtube.com/watch?v=2L4B-Vpvx1A&t=3s
- A lovely story of building something beautiful from something that is waste: "Landfill Harmonic – the 'Recycled Orchestra'." https://www.youtube.com/watch?v=yYbORpgSmjg
- A short video explaining the impact of e-waste: "By the numbers: Impact of e-waste" (ABC News). https://www.youtube.com/watch?v=3VkpXLuDmX8

## Example 2: Driverless cars

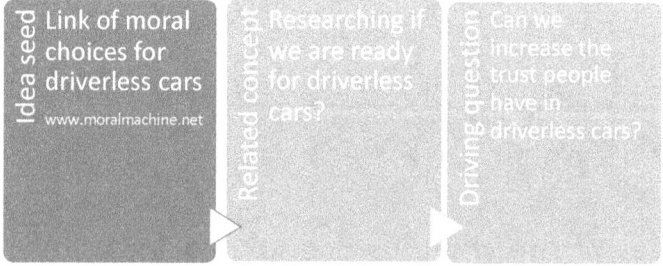

**Idea seed:** Link of moral choices for driverless cars www.moralmachine.net

**Related concept:** Researching if we are ready for driverless cars?

**Driving question:** Can we increase the trust people have in driverless cars?

**Related resources**
- An ethical debate around driverless cars: "Driverless, autonomous cars present ethical challenges — so how do we write the laws?" (ABC News). https://www.abc.net.au/news/2018-07-05/driverless-cars-ethical-debate-you-decide/9836786

- Fully self-driving cars: "Waymo's fully autonomous driving technology is here." https://www.youtube.com/watch?v=aaOB-ErYq6Y
- "Are we ready for driverless cars?" PBS NewsHour Classroom. https://www.pbs.org/newshour/classroom/posts/2013/05/are-we-ready-for-driverless-cars

## Example 3: Promoting the wellbeing of indigenous cultures

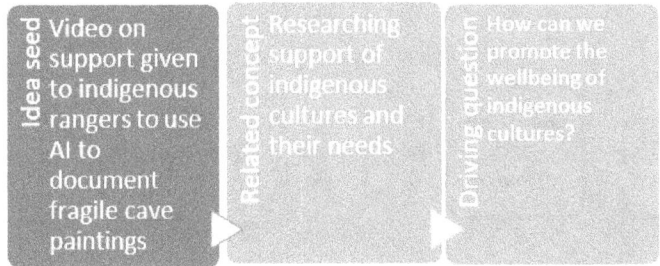

Idea seed: Video on support given to indigenous rangers to use AI to document fragile cave paintings

Related concept: Researching support of indigenous cultures and their needs

Driving question: How can we promote the wellbeing of indigenous cultures?

**Related resources**
- Artificial intelligence being used to document cave paintings: "Artificial intelligence helps catalogue Aboriginal rock art in Far North Queensland" (ABC News). https://www.abc.net.au/news/2023-09-15/artificial-intelligence-rock-art-far-north-queensland-indigenous/102851802
- "Our knowledge, our way." Indigenous science (CSIRO). https://www.csiro.au/en/research/indigenous-science

CHAPTER 7

# Brainstorm and research

As I write this section, an image from my childhood pops into my mind. It highlights why brainstorming and research are so essential.

I grew up in a seaside town and would walk my dog all over the town. In a yard one block from the beach, a man was building a boat. "Not unusual or unexpected," I hear you say. Well, no, this boat was different. It was about 8 metres long, on a metal rebar frame, and was made from cement. Even at a young age I can remember thinking "That is going to sink". I wondered at the time if he had tried a smaller version first, or if he had investigated what makes boats float.

After 10-odd years of seeing this "boat" develop, the hull was moved the 50 metres to the dock via trailer. I would like to tell you a good news story and say that I had been incorrect.

But no. It sank. No surprise there. I guess that he went back to the drawing board. But it does confirm (I nearly said cement) in my mind the importance of research, prototyping and problem-solving.

Once the stimulus has been viewed and discussed, it is time to begin research. While questions are provided within the assessment document, it is ideal if students develop several questions within their group to extend understanding and research. This helps to promote ownership and deeper understanding of the project. This in turn contributes to successful completion of the project.

Questions can be general, such as "What is green technology?" but could also focus on responses to the stimuli provided.

Questions in the **innovative sustainable products** task are shown below:
1. Name two pieces of information that stood out for you from these videos.
2. What is sustainability?
3. Identify two businesses that create sustainable products.
4. What makes these businesses different and special (this is called "point of difference")?
5. Is there a point of difference that you think these businesses have overlooked?

By researching information on similar concepts or businesses, it is possible to gain insight into how to move forward. Developing skills to work out the businesses' point of difference will help students to understand the way that businesses or concepts work.

An excellent way to create meaningful experiences is to have a subject expert participate in the program. This could be a face-to-face, videoed or online (e.g. Zoom) experience. To prepare to speak to mentors, it would be ideal for the students to come up with at least three questions before any meetings take place.

Examples of questions for business-related mentors might be:

- What makes your business unique?
- Why did you begin your business (relating back to Simon Sinek's video)?
- What is your favourite aspect of your business?
- Is there an area you would like to extend further?
- Is there something that is holding you back from progressing with that extension area?

Examples of questions for concept mentors might be:

- When building earthquake-proof buildings, what would be the essential components?
- What are the biggest problems caused by microplastics?
- What are some ways that microplastics enter the water cycle initially?

## Summary of key points

- Create a question that is open to multiple interpretations and end points.
- The question should engage students to want to solve the problem at hand.
- Select stimuli that spark creativity and further questions.
- Add simple research questions that get to the heart of the issue.
- When possible, include a mentor or subject expert in the initial stages.

## Building group dynamics

As educators, we all know that students want to work with their friends, so they have someone to laugh with or procrastinate with. These groupings can be fine for simple tasks and tasks with highly structured guidelines. Group work can have varying levels of success, but as Baber (2021) suggests, effective group work "enhances critical thinking by engaging higher order thinking skills". Group work can also support effective educational practices, because "interactive engagement may allow students to build their understanding beyond that of any individual because of the complementary knowledge of the members" (Dutta & Rangnekar, 2022).

The problem with this type of grouping is that students tend to want to be what they have always been and do what they have always done. The key purpose of the Authentic STEAM Framework is to encourage students to reach their potential, to step out of their comfort zones and see the excitement and fulfilment that can come from achieving in a different way with different people. "Student-selected groups versus instructor-selected groups did not affect student performance. Moreover, by providing students with comfortable learning conditions, we may reduce their anxiety and fear of failure and eventually improve their emotional well-being" (Gajderowicz et al., 2023).

However, less natural groupings can produce more successful outcomes. While there are ways that groupings may need to be managed, to reduce known friction between some students, this can be resolved through teacher experience and understanding of group dynamics. Random groupings are worth exploring, as they give students who might not otherwise shine a chance to do so.

Random groupings have provided joyous and unexpected results time and again with this framework. One of the key issues with many traditional educational experiences is that students who do not achieve well within these experiences continue to be unsuccessful. The beauty of a STEAM environment is that students who might have manifested behavioural issues in traditional classroom environments not only participate fully but become leaders in this type of learning experience.

Why? Because not having to fit the mould of a traditional student gives them a chance to show their creativity and lateral thinking. While this may get them into trouble elsewhere, it is the very thing that promotes success in the STEAM environment. It does take courage and some redirection on occasion, but overall the results and positive effects are worth the effort required.

## Creating a team

Creating a team is not as simple as putting students in groups. There is no guarantee from this framework that those students will then work effectively together. There is always the possibility that one or two students will complete the work while others stand by.

There are several reasons for this. Students who are high achievers can often feel the need to hold up and support the group, which can cause resentment. On the flip side, lower achievers may feel that they do not have a defined role within the group. Successful use of the Authentic STEAM Framework can decrease these issues, as it places some rules and structures within the group narrative. It also makes the process more egalitarian, and the work more equally distributed.

The keys to this are role allocation and accountability. Step one in this process is setting up assigned roles within the group that each student takes responsibility for. These roles can include but are not limited to:

- Team manager
- Design team
- Building team
- Creative musical team
- Timekeeper and administrator.

It is important to use the appropriate roles for the relevant tasks, as these will differ on each occasion. It may be also possible for one student to have many roles, depending on the challenge. The breakdown of these roles is summarised in the table below:

| Role | Responsibility |
| --- | --- |
| Team manager | Manages the project and co-ordinates with other members of the team to bring out the best within the team |
| Design team | Focuses on the artistic aspects of the challenge – e.g. logos, banners, packaging and visual aesthetics of the prototypes |
| Building team | Creates any props, stalls or prototypes, in conjunction with the design team |
| Creative musical team | Creates any music or audio that is required for the project |
| Timekeeper and administrator | Works with the team manager to create a plan for completing the tasks, then ensures that timeframes are adhered to; does some general administration if needed |

While it is important for all students to feel that they have a role, it is also important that they feel they have a voice in the team, and that their voice is heard. Some ways to do that involve having some strong guidelines around questioning – how to question, when to question, and the way to question. This will be covered in more detail later in the chapter.

## Summary of key points

- Students of all abilities can show their potential to become leaders.
- Group roles and dynamics are essential.
- Appropriate questioning – by yourself and the students – is essential for success.

## Brainstorming

Brainstorming is a key concept in the success of this framework. By focusing on having no limits or expectations about where the process will take you and your students, this allows end points to be expanded and the creative process to be increased.

As indicated in the previous section, one of the key concepts for brainstorming success is to focus on the *Why?*

- *Why* are we doing this?
- *Why* would changing the design add to the customer experience?

When facilitating these projects, asking *Why?* and then getting students to question and focus on their own *Why?* can be your key involvement and support.

As a facilitator, guiding ideas and encouraging students to further question themselves or extend their ideas is the best way to help support them. The key concept is:

> There is no such thing as a bad idea – even the craziest options could end up as a part of the final solution.

So, embrace the crazy. Write that weird idea down and see how it could work or be adapted to solve the challenge. On the latest occasion the question above ("How do we work with Tasmanian quality produce to create a unique and innovative product?") was posed, the responses included:

- Bath bombs and soaps made from the rejected berries to save on food waste.
- A mushroom recipe book made from mushroom paper. The paper was impregnated with seeds that could be used in the recipes and packaged with salts and other products. The paper was biodegradable and could be composted.
- An eggshell exfoliating soap made from waste products returned to the farm. By returning shells, you receive a discount on your next order.
- A website that showcases organic pork and other organically produced Tasmanian produce monthly, and provides recipes and food packs to promote Tasmanian businesses.
- A business that uses organic beef in healthy lunch packs or party platters.

All of these were great ideas emerging from the original question. This is amazing considering that the students' average age was 12. Some of their initial ideas were interesting, and so outside of the box that they could not even see the box. Within a few hours, some groups had three or four viable options to choose from.

However, the demise of the "beef soap" idea was not a sadness. As one of the students said, "Very creative, but who wants to smell like MEAT!"

On the flip side, the initial focus for the students working on the mushroom recipe book was to make mushroom shoes. Not ideal. But this then morphed into a conversation about what might work, which resulted in the amazing mushroom paper recipe book.

## Effective facilitator responses

Some key questions to promote discussion and facilitate deeper responses from students are:

- Great thinking! If you do not think it works, how could you adjust it slightly to make the product/process work better?
- How could you expand that to look at it differently?
- What *does* work about that idea? Let us ask your teammates what it makes them think of when you discuss this.
- Where could you look to find a possible solution?

### The story of Play-Doh

When coal was the primary source of heat within homes and left smoky marks inside, Joe McVickers owned a company that produced a wallpaper-cleaning product. Once people started to change to oil, Joe started losing money. That was until his sister-in-law – a nursery schoolteacher – suggested that it might be great for her students to play and model with.

Joe added colours to it, and changed the marketing, and Play-Doh was born. This story is a reminder that many ideas are just a small adjustment away from being amazing.

I use this story as a reminder when I feel discouraged. Continue to embrace your weird and wonderful ideas.

It might be a small adjustment that can make a great big difference.

CHAPTER 8

# Design and simplify

A great way to kick-start the brainstorming and selection process is using a poster or whiteboard, along with Post-it notes for ideas and stickers or markers for voting. Students are given sticky notes initially to write ideas on, and these are placed on a board. No idea is out of bounds. However, it is often good to set a time limit, as a small amount of time pressure seems to improve focus.

Students can showcase their favourite option, which gives them a chance to develop their ideas even further. Once the showcasing is complete, students will be able to vote on which are their favourite options. They can use one or more stickers to vote, and then the top two or three can be chosen. Removal of the other options gives a chance to focus on the chosen ones.

Retreating to individual computers and spending some time researching, using the questions listed within the workbook, allows students who *didn't* come up with the idea to develop ownership of that idea. It also helps with tangential thinking and the development of the product/design ideas. This process will take the solution down from three to two, and then from two to one main solution or design.

The use of the stickers and Post-it notes is also key to the evaluation of the product. A sample board might look like the one below:

To place some structure into the brainstorming, the following steps work well:

1. Brainstorm similar products/solutions to problems that already exist.
2. Brainstorm further products/solutions that do not exist that you could create.
3. Use stickers to vote on which *two* ideas you would like to look at in further detail.
4. Decide which *two* products you feel are worthy of further research.
5. Within the group, for each of the two possible options, discuss:
    - What works well?
    - What could work better?
6. What are some modifications you could make to improve the product?
7. Decide on your first choice of product.

Please remind students to keep their remarks positive when discussing other people's ideas and to focus on the specific questions above in each case.

## Summary of key points

- Ensure students have roles within the group.
- No ideas are wrong or crazy – they could just be a starting point.
- Encourage and model speaking positively.
- Focus on steps within the brainstorming to lead to a final product idea.
- Build ownership of the project through research.

## Your target customer

### Definition of a target customer

A target customer is the person who would be most likely to buy your product. For example, which group might be most likely to buy a custom-designed surfboard? The process of creating target customers is detailed below. While this is not a standard part of teaching practice, this component is one of the most successful and integral pieces of the Authentic STEAM Framework.

Focusing on designing for a specific customer gives clarity to the concept and design. Be very specific about who you are designing for.

It is important to continually refer students back to the target customer and design for them, as this brings focus and clarity to the concept and allows redirection back to the task in a positive way.

One of the key components of the Authentic STEAM Framework is the focus on target customers. To solve any problem, whether completing a task or designing a product, it is more productive to focus on a specific person or group of people. It then becomes easier to make decisions for that person. As a result, the final product is more effective, creative and deeply thought out.

The importance of this step cannot be underestimated. Students (and adults) "have a tendency to want to create based on their own experiences and what they are fond of". They will often need to be reminded that "their job as designers was to create something beneficial for their end user" (Lee, 2018). By focusing on the target customer, the natural bias that can exist when designing for one's own pleasure and interest can be eradicated. As a facilitator, the constant question needs to be: "What would your target customer need/want?"

### Creating target customers

To be successful at creating target customers, it is important to deep-dive into who the person is, what they look like, and what their interests are. Be specific and give detail. Either draw or find an image online that can be used to define your target customer.

The important questions to ask to define the target customer are:

1. Who might we be producing a product for?
    - What age are they?
    - What are their needs?

- What do they want from their products?
- What don't they want?
- How much money/time/patience/skill etc. do they have?

2. Give the person a name, gender, clothing, job, and so on that will make you feel like they are a real person you are creating a product for. Draw an image of that person that you can refer to throughout the design thinking process.

In defining the target customer for a custom surfboard, the specific question that would need to be asked is:

> Who might want to buy a custom surfboard?

Here is an example of some responses to this question:

> It might be out of reach for a teenager but might suit someone who has just started work and wants to treat themselves in some way. Alternatively, this could be an older professional person who loved surfing in their youth and wants to get back into it.

There are many different options. They key is to pick one – nothing is incorrect. It is just a focus for the design process. Detailed below is a sample target customer for the custom surfboard.

> Tyrone lived at the beach when he was a teenager and surfed every day after school and all through the weekend. He is 25 and works in a department store. He has received a recent promotion to manager. To celebrate his promotion, he would like to buy a custom surfboard – something that could be hung in his house to remind him of his teen years but could also be used whenever he gets the chance to surf.
>
> He has some surfboards from when he was younger, but now he wants something that he can brag to his friends about. He does not want something that is the same as everyone else's. He has good skills on a surfboard but is a bit rusty. He hopes this will be the excuse to get started again with surfing and improve his fitness.
>
> He is prepared to spend up for the right board – something custom-made specifically for him.
>
> Tyrone wears a shirt and tie during the week but dresses in board shorts and tank top at the weekend. He is embracing the idea of working hard but playing hard and getting a work/life balance.

## Expanding to other target customers

The process of creating target customers then leads into designing prototypes. Once the initial prototype has been completed, then it is useful to expand the range of target customers to extend the prototype. In other words:

> Who else might like this product?

Here are some examples of other target customers that could be created once the initial target customer has been created and designed for:

- The parents of a child who is about to have an 18th or 21st who want to buy a "special" birthday present. Don and Debbie want to buy a present for their 21-year-old son, David, who is surf mad and very hard to buy for.
- Peter, who is in the grip of a midlife crisis. He is an executive who has money to burn but has never surfed and is looking to regain his youth.
- Aaron, a hipster who can surf and enjoys it, but wants to be seen to have something unique and "bespoke" – made especially for him and no-one else.

All these target customer proposals would need to be expanded more but would give a different focus for the new prototypes that are being created.

CHAPTER 9

# Prototype and refine

## Prototypes

A prototype is a sample of a product or design that is created with the target customer in mind. This is where all the design thinking comes into fruition. It focuses on expanding the vision to include variations within the original prototype.

It is still essential to keep the target customer in mind and design for what they want or need. Some of the thinking for our previous example is shown below:

> What would the target customer like to see within this product/design?
> - What are the features that the target customer would appreciate and be attracted to?
> - What are the most important components for the target customer?
> - What would be some variations that would work for this target customer?
> - What are other variations that would appeal to our expanded target customer profile?

Prototypes can be created in electronic form, or on paper, but students will often prefer to build a three-dimensional model of their prototype and its variations. These can be in any form, from paper or cardboard to plasticine or clay. The form the prototype takes is not essential, as long as it represents what the product or solution entails effectively.

When presenting the prototype, it is essential to be able to relate the final product back to the target customer and be able to provide a comprehensive explanation of what its features are and how they meet the needs and requirements that were set out initially.

## Variations

Variations are small changes that give multiple options to the target customer for the product or design that might appeal to them. A prime example is the purchase of running shoes. These will have a basic design, but there will be several variations in colour, branding, etc. that might appeal to different target customers. Variations allow for choice, and choice will increase the chances of successful completion of the project.

### Tyrone's surfboard designs with variations

What would Tyrone want his surfboard to look like?

Tyrone is stylish and follows many clothing and design trends. But he is also nostalgic. He wants something with a modern twist, but also something that reminds him of his teen years when surfing was such a major part of his life.

So, his design should focus on similarities to his 1980s surfboard style, with minimal changes to the shape, but with colours and patterns that have a retro style with a modern twist. Some possible samples are shown below:

## Refining ideas

At the point where prototypes and variations have been developed, it is time again to *refine* what has been produced. To do that, revisit your target customer and ask relevant questions:

- Have we produced products that the target customer wants, needs and would buy and use?
- Would our colours, styles and ideas meet what is required?

Coco Chanel is famous for saying "Before you leave the house, look in the mirror and take at least one thing off". This concept is true for the refinement process as well. Look at what has been produced, then remove something, whether it be a full sample or part thereof.

More is not necessarily better. By reviewing as a team what has been produced, and refining what is being presented, you will make the overall look that much more effective.

## Deliverables

Deliverables are a name for the components that will need to be included in the final presentation. These components will be discussed below, with a detailed set of instructions on simple ways that these components can be completed. While there is not just one way to create deliverables, the instructions given have been found to be useful in the past.

The deliverables have been broken down into standard and extension tasks. Not all these tasks will need to be completed for all topics, as they will not fit into every project.

### Standard

- Business or project name
- Logos and banners
- Jingle (audio)
- Advertisement (video)
- Prototypes and variations
- Shopfront.

### Extended

- Website
- App
- Cost analysis (Excel)
- 3D modelling via ThingLink.

Below are some more details and basic guidelines for each of these deliverables. Companion videos for many of the components will explain further and give visual representations of the information required.

## Further details on types of deliverables

|  | Standard |
|---|---|
| **Business or project name** | The business name or concept name is key to producing the product. Depending on the type of challenge, the name might not be used in the wider picture but is useful in concept- and design-building. |
| **Logos and banners** | A logo is an effective way to bring overarching coverage to the whole design thinking process. Not only does it give a visual representation of what is being represented but it can help with colour concepts and prototype design. |
|  | There are many websites and programs that can be used to create logos. Canva (https://www.canva.com) is one of the tools that can provide simple yet professional examples of banners and logos. It provides sample sizes, templates, text samples, images and shapes. It also allows images to be copied and pasted to be used as part of logos. Components are easily downloadable and modifiable. |
|  | In terms of what makes effective logos and banners, the following guidelines are useful:<br>• Use three or less colours – colours should be directly relatable to the product they are selling.<br>• Use two or less fonts.<br>• Colours and fonts should be seen throughout any presentation that is produced, in order to create an identifiable corporate look |
| **Jingle (audio)** | A jingle or catchphrase is useful to bring focus to a product. This can be included in the final presentation or can be incorporated as part of the advertisement video. |
|  | The jingle should be less than 30 seconds long and should encompass the project or business's core concepts or ideas. |
|  | The Voice Recorder app available on most computers works well. In terms of creating strong voice recordings:<br>• If possible, use a separate microphone for better clarity of sound.<br>• Use a quiet space where interruptions and outside noises will not be heard. |

| | |
|---|---|
| **Advertisement (video)** | Many of the same concepts apply to video as to audio.<br><br>When creating the advertisement, students need to work on scripting and content before filming. This way they can focus on the specifics of what needs to be said.<br><br>Concepts to keep in mind:<br><br>• The video should be 2–3 minutes long.<br>• Make sure that lighting is bright and consistent.<br>• Sound quality needs to be good. |
| **Prototypes and variations** | Prototypes can be drawn or designed, but can also be produced from cardboard, paper, wood or any other product. They can also be produced in a 3D-modelling program such as Autodesk Fusion 360.<br><br>Initially products should be designed on paper, with different colours, sizes, patterns, etc. being developed. If possible, create mock-ups of as many variations as possible. |
| **Shopfront** | A shopfront is a space where products and information can be presented together in one space. This could just be a table, but can be decorated with logos, banners, packaging and prototypes. It is the overall representation of the product or concept and needs to be as cohesive as possible. |

| | |
|---|---|
| **Extended** | |
| **Website** | There are many web-builders that allow creation of simple websites and have templates available for quicker completion. Two that come to mind are https://www.godaddy.com and https://www.wix.com.<br><br>Key components of successful websites:<br><br>• Think about what the viewer of the website wants to see rather than what you want to tell them.<br>• Simplify the number of pages and have the most important pages on the left.<br>• Minimise how much scrolling from the top of the page viewers need to do.<br>• Keep consistency with colours and fonts to match logos and banners.<br>• Use simple fonts such as Arial, Helvetica, Calibri and Verdana, which were all created with on-screen viewing in mind.<br>• Do not use underlining, as it is often confused with hyperlinks. |

| | |
|---|---|
| **App** | Simple and free app builders are available to use, and many of the same rules for websites apply to apps. Examples of simple app-builders include https://www.appypie.com and https://jotform.com. |
| **Flyer** | While this is now a less-used concept in marketing and design, it is still useful for final display and presentations. |
| | A flyer can be created in Word using columns and needs to be completed in the same style as any logos or banners. |
| **Cost analysis (Excel)** | Excel is useful for basic cost breakdown if it is needed. Spreadsheets should have minimal fonts and formatting, as the numbers should speak for themselves. |
| | Spreadsheets should be longer than they are wide for easy reading. |
| **ThingLink** | ThingLink is a great interactive product and can be found at https://www.thinglink.com. This is a free product and allows videos, images, websites, quizzes and various other links to be presented in creative ways. It is a great option for use with augmented reality and virtual reality goggles. |

CHAPTER 10

# Present and evaluate

Coming up with an overall vision for a project or task will often mean incorporating deliverables such as a logo, a name, audio, video, packaging, etc. to add to the final presentation.

## Marketing and design

The marketing and design component is the one that mostly focuses on the "A" in STEAM. Educators who are comfortable in STEM education often comment that the art component is the one that is most terrifying to them. However, it is the overarching component that makes all the other components come together in a more cohesive way. Because this is an area of concern, many resources and support videos have been provided to help educators embrace the "A" in STEAM.

If the marketing and design concept is solid, it provides a framework for how all the other elements work together. The initial focus, however, needs to be:

> How could we use our designs to market our concept to customers?

This marketing may be in the form of advertisements and logos, but could also include the websites, apps and other products mentioned previously.

Once again, "People don't buy what we do, they buy why we do it" (Sinek, 2009).

So, the key to successful marketing is to find a concept that all members of the group can get behind and believe in – a predominant reason why their design or product is relevant.

## The final presentation

The final presentation is the way in which all concepts are brought together into one concept. A "Final Pitch" style presentation works well, but this can also be done successfully using PowerPoint and presenting the key components in this format. For those students who are concerned about presenting to a group, a pre-recorded video is a great way to complete the task to a high level.

Some key components of a successful presentation are:

- First focus on the *Why?*
- More information is not better. A 2–3-minute presentation or video is ideal.
- A clear and concise presentation helps to showcase the approach, the design, and the final solution.

Using the presentation approach is a great way for students to build trust in their own capabilities. Not all students within the group need to speak at the final presentation, but all should have input into the final product. Using the presentation allows individuals to gain confidence. As the presentation is developed, students should be encouraged to work as concisely as possible to get their point across.

### Summary of key points

- Focus on the *Why?*
- Create prototypes that suit the needs and wants of your target customer.
- Create variations that suit the needs and wants of a wider audience.
- Create an overall design and look that makes your design pop.
- Create concise and easy-to-understand presentations that get to the point and showcase your design or product.

# Authentic STEAM Framework template

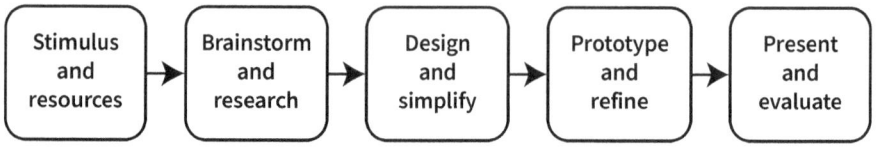

| | |
|---|---|
| **Challenge** | Type challenge question here |
| **Microlearning** | *Getting started* |
| **Stimulus and resources** | Insert stimulus image here to get conversation started<br>Insert resources here, including web links |
| **Microlearning** | *Target customer*<br>*Beginning design* |
| **Brainstorm and research** | Include some questions as starting points |
| **Microlearning** | *Further design*<br>*Prototyping and variations* |
| **Design and simplify** | Space to design and create<br>Begin to narrow down choices |
| **Microlearning** | *Presentation*<br>*Evaluation* |
| **Prototype and refine** | Finalise choices for selection<br>Begin simulations by creating samples and testing |
| **Microlearning** | *Presentation*<br>*Evaluation* |
| **Present and evaluate** | Presentation key points<br>Evaluating the solution – peer- and self-assessment. |

# PART 3
# DESIGNING AUTHENTIC EXAMPLES

"Anyone who has never made a mistake has never tried something new".
– ALBERT EINSTEIN

The focus for educators is often on producing course content assessment tasks quickly and efficiently. We do not always have the luxury of sufficient time to produce exactly what we want to produce, and tasks often take two or more iterations to get to a place that we are happy with.

We are also tasked with teaching effectively a group of diverse learners with different needs, abilities and experiences. This means that assessment tasks need to give each student the ability to shine in their own way.

An effective way to do this is to create learning experiences and assessment tasks that are open-ended and can be interpreted in as many ways as imagination will allow. The Authentic STEAM Framework allows students and educators alike to consolidate and extend learning in positive and creative ways.

This section will cover the creation of examples that use the Authentic STEAM Framework, as well as showing several examples of the framework and where it fits into the curriculum. Finally, it will also showcase some simple skills (called "microlearnings") that work in tandem with the framework to empower educators and students alike to succeed. These are available from STEAMauthenticity.com.

## CHAPTER 11

# Building resources

## Before beginning

Building relationships is essential in creating strong educational experiences. How can a child be taught effectively if we do not know who they are, how they think, and what they need? This is a difficult concept with large classes but is essential in effectively educating and supporting our students.

> Every child wants to be seen, heard, known and understood, and that is the best gift you can give them. It is also the way to get them to achieve at their best.
>
> This approach to learning can give every child the chance to shine.

Is this framework going to magically create innovative, intrinsically motivated learners?

*No.*

But does working this way give students the chance to be themselves, showcase their strengths, and develop their creativity?

*Yes, it does.*

This is something to think about as we move into designing assessments.

## Creating effective driving questions

There are many ways in which questions can be built for resources, and this component can be one of the most time-consuming parts of the whole process. The reason for this is that getting the question correct and creating something that is open to interpretation in a positive way is not as easy as one might think.

A good question has several aims, the first of which is an understanding of your educational purpose and learning intention. A strong question will allow for critical thinking and problem-solving. Clarity of purpose is essential – what do you wish to achieve, and what do you want your students to gain from this experience?

Learning the curriculum for short-term knowledge gain is not a true purpose. However, deepening learning and developing skills that allow students to gain long-term transfer of content and be able to relate that content to real-world understanding is a true purpose.

Open-ended questions are the quickest path to developing tasks that will help students to develop the critical thinking required to be an effective 21st-century learner. Closed questions such as "What is the capital of Indonesia?" require prior knowledge and have only one response. Open questions such as:

> "If you had committed a crime, would you allow artificial intelligence to determine your jail sentence?"

open avenues for research, a detailed discussion, and many different interpretations of the original question.

Such open questions also promote further questions, such as:

- How do judges determine what a reasonable sentence is?
- Are they consistent in their sentencing?
- What if the judge is biased against me?
- Is there a list of past sentences for the crime I have committed?
- Would a chatbot using artificial intelligence be able to give me the death sentence?
- Is there a point at which I would like a human to step in; if so, what would that point be?

The language of the question is essential for a successful outcome in this process. Questions that need to be asked are:

- Is the wording clear and age-appropriate?
- Can it be discussed with minimal input from the facilitator?
- Is it too vague?

One way to ensure these requirements are met is to seek guidance from other educators in your team and ask how they interpret the open-ended question. This will allow you to interpret and modify the question if needed before using it in the classroom.

Another strategy that can be used is to present the question or task to a group of students and ask them to be your guinea pigs. This may sound strange, but giving students the chance to critique your work without sanction often creates a learning experience that forges deeper relationships and more effective learning experiences. Gaining feedback and improving questions is an essential part of the process.

While it may be human nature to have ideas in mind for the completion of any task, influencing students with your own agenda is not part of an effective process. Keeping the question open-ended allows for creative interpretations that will bring vastly more creative outcomes.

## Scaffolding with strong stimuli

As we have seen, an educational stimulus is content that evokes a response for further research and discussion. Examples of stimuli could be a video, an image, a case study, a subject specialist, or a physical item. They are often directly related to the question provided but can be tangential to promote a questioning response. Having stimuli not directly related to the task can promote interesting responses, but this path needs to be chosen carefully.

It is essential that the audience is considered when creating stimuli. Language, interests and skills should be considered and, when possible, should cater for the age group, abilities and interests of the intended audience.

Creating something that is directly relatable to students will challenge them to do, be and create more than they have ever done. The key to a strong stimulus is to find something that extends thinking and encourages students to take risks to create something amazing.

## Encouraging students to build their own driving questions and stimuli

Encouraging students to build their own projects is an ideal way to promote and develop their critical thinking skills. Ideally, they would have been part of project-based learning challenges using the Authentic STEAM Framework before.

This will give the students the base upon which to build their own questions. Initially, they may need some guidance, but eventually they will be able to create research questions effectively, a skill which will be useful within subsequent education and work environments.

Initially, providing students with examples of strong research questions will help them to gain understanding of what is required. They then need to work out what they would like to research, and practise composing that into a question. With guidance, they can then mould that into a question that is concise, rather than too broad or vague.

Once that has been defined, facilitate deeper thinking through prompts or guiding questions. Some examples of guiding questions could be:

- What excites you about this topic?
- Is there a problem you would like to research within this topic?
- Is there an end point of measurable information you are trying to find?
- What problem might this research solve?

Students regularly say "I am interested in…" Our role as educators is to then pivot that interest area into something that can be researched or evaluated in many ways. For example:

> **Student:** "I would like to create a women's soccer shoe."
>
> **Educator:** Turn the response into researching women's sport and how it has grown.
> - What are the differences between male sport and female sport?
> - Talk to mentors and female sports people.
> - Research their issues with existing clothing.
> - Create a design or series of designs that will solve those issues.
>
> The question might be:
>
> "How can we research existing sports clothing and equipment to create equipment that will meet the needs of female athletes?"

Finally, once the basic question has been refined, get the students to focus on researching their topic to review and revise the issues. This will help them to hone their ideas into the best form of question possible.

Using artificial intelligence programs such as ChatGPT can be a useful tool to help mentor students to develop their own driving questions. ChatGPT can be seen as a third person in the room – it can be used to put keywords and concepts into the process, and then iterate to get to a final point of questioning.

## Setting up your template

Within this section is a general template for content creation. Blank sections have been removed to prevent wasted space, but all concepts are there. Examples of completed challenges will be shown below.

## [Name of Challenge] STEAM Challenge

| | |
|---|---|
| **Challenge** | Driving question here |
| **Microlearning** | *Getting started* |
| **Stimulus and resources** | Quote or short stimulus here<br><br>Relevant resources here |
| **Microlearning** | *Target customer*<br><br>*Beginning design* |
| **Brainstorm and research** | Design and draw your target customer. What do they look like? What are they interested in? Include name, gender, clothing, work, etc.<br><br>Design your brainstorming and research around what your target customer would like.<br><br>• Relevant questions to aid research here<br><br>Use the space provided on the following pages of this booklet to show your target customer and research details. |

## Target customer design

More space is provided on actual template – this is shortened to remove extra white space.

## Research details

More space is provided on actual template – this is shortened to remove extra white space.

| Microlearning | Further design |
| --- | --- |
| | Prototyping and variations |
| Design and simplify | How will you present your response? Create several designs and then work out with your group which response would work best for your target customer. Place details in the space provided in this booklet |
| Prototype and refine | Create prototypes, then… |

## Design creation

More space is provided on actual template – this is shortened to remove extra white space.

| Microlearning | Presentation |
| --- | --- |
| | Evaluation |

## Presentation details

More space is provided on actual template – this is shortened to remove extra white space.

| Present and evaluate | Presentation key points |
| --- | --- |
| | Evaluating the solution – peer- and self-assessment |

## CHAPTER 12

# Authentic examples

Within this chapter are some examples of stimuli that have been built using the Authentic STEAM Framework. Basic structure and components are given for these examples, with full versions made available online. These examples are all designed to be longer-term projects over multiple lessons or challenge sessions. They will have more complex research and design and presentation requirements. For shorter-term challenges, see the examples in **Part 4: The Simplified STEAM Framework**.

## Example 1: Holding back the tides

| Question | Can we create a product that will reduce the erosion of coastal land? |
|---|---|
| **Supports content** | Climate change, geology |
| **Learning areas** | Science, engineering |
| **Research questions** | • What is erosion?<br>• What are the causes of erosion of coastal land?<br>• How does it affect coastal land?<br>• What are some ways in which coastal erosion is already being reduced? Discuss their relative effectiveness. |
| **Stimulus** | • Coastal erosion video:<br>"Beach erosion causes Outer Banks homes to fall into ocean."<br>https://www.youtube.com/watch?v=byQY1TGcMIE<br>• Living shorelines:<br>"'Living shorelines' may help mitigate future climate damage."<br>https://www.youtube.com/watch?v=NDBVyUmRgeg<br>• Barriers for beach erosion:<br>"Projects underway to prevent future beach erosion on the Treasure Coast."<br>https://www.youtube.com/watch?v=hM2Bs5TakNY |

| | |
|---|---|
| Deliverables | • Name of company and logo<br>• Multiple prototypes of solutions<br>• Pitch-style demo and marketing |
| Microlearning | • Logo design<br>• Video skills |

## Example 2: Reimagining unused spaces

| | |
|---|---|
| **Question** | **How can we reimagine unused spaces?** |
| Supports content | Engineering, sustainability, creativity |
| Stimulus | "Have nothing in your houses that you do not know to be beautiful or believe to be useful" – William Morris. |
| Learning areas | Science, art, engineering, digital technology, design technology |
| Research questions | • What have others done to fix up neglected spaces?<br>• Should spaces be useful or beautiful, or can they be both?<br>• Are there any unused or under-utilised spaces within our school or general community?<br>• What are the needs of our school and community that are not being met or met effectively?<br>• What could you create that might enhance or update the space?<br>• How might it enhance how useful or beautiful the space is? |
| Deliverables | • Name of the space and sign<br>• Visual representation or model of the project<br>• Multiple sample prototypes of solutions<br>• Video-pitch presentation of final solution |
| Microlearning | • Canva or design<br>• Video editing |

Some example outcomes used by this stimulus:
- A Zen space within the school environment
- A space to support the homeless community
- A community garden space for the school community
- A mural to enhance a school space and support student wellbeing.

## Example 3: Creating a chatbot

| Question | Can we create a chatbot to solve a simple problem? |
|---|---|
| Supports content | Digital technology, computational thinking, algorithm design, creativity, problem-solving |
| Stimulus | "Chatbots are important because you will not feel stupid asking important questions. Sometimes talking to someone can be a bit intimidating. Talking to a chatbot makes that a lot easier!" (Petter Bae Brandtzaeg).<br><br>Dan Shewan: "10 of the most innovative chatbots on the web". https://www.wordstream.com/blog/ws/chatbots |
| Research questions | • What are chatbots and where are they currently used?<br>• What are some examples of products that can build chatbots?<br>• Can/should chatbots replace human interaction? |
| Deliverables | • Chatbot name and image<br>• Data flow diagram of chatbot structure<br>• Simple chatbot creation<br>• Video "Final Pitch" presentation of final solution |
| Microlearning | • Mind maps<br>• Creating your first chatbot |

Some example outcomes used by this stimulus:

- What is the correct pet for you and your family?
- What are the best subjects for me?
- Where should we go on holiday?

A note of caution with this task: make sure that the question that is being used is simple, as students will discover how complex some issues are. Paper-based is best first, as it allows the complexity to be analysed before beginning the computer-based solution.

## Example 4: Homelessness

| Question | Should housing be a human right? |
|---|---|
| Supports content | Current social context, building and design, creativity |
| Stimulus | "We have come dangerously close to accepting the homeless situation as a problem that we just can't solve" (Linda Lingle).<br><br>"Making it so you don't have to look at homeless people isn't a solution to homelessness" (Sara Luterman). |

| | |
|---|---|
| Research questions | • What is homelessness?<br>• What are the main reasons why people are homeless?<br>• What are homelessness statistics in Australia?<br>• What different forms does homelessness take?<br>• What are some examples of efforts made to decrease homelessness?<br>• How successful have these efforts been? |
| Deliverables | • Short story or video explaining research<br>• Various proposals for possible solutions<br>• Scale model of solution if appropriate |
| Microlearning | Excel introduction for costings |

Some sample outcomes that could be created by this stimulus:
- Reuse of abandoned spaces for housing
- Relocatable "tiny homes"
- Market gardens and fruit trees in unused spaces for supporting the homeless community.

## Example 5: Sustainability

| | |
|---|---|
| Question | Can we create a product that helps to promote and improve sustainable practices? |
| Supports content | Sustainability, creativity |
| Stimulus | "The greatest threat to our planet is the belief that someone else will save it" (Robert Swan).<br><br>Leyla Acaroglu: "Sustainability is not what you think it is". https://www.youtube.com/watch?v=hViHEPPPXK8<br><br>Small World Journeys: "Aboriginal Sustainability". https://www.youtube.com/watch?v=Bi_sKQsfCLo |
| Research questions | • What is sustainability?<br>• How much waste do Australians produce per year?<br>• What are the different types of waste?<br>• How is this waste dealt with?<br>• Research products that reduce waste<br>• Research products that are produced from waste products |
| Deliverables | • A prototype of a product that either reduces waste or reuses a waste product<br>• A video showcasing the product |
| Microlearning | Video editing |

Some sample outcomes that could be created by this stimulus:
- A fridge that messages you with recipes to reduce food waste
- A washing machine that recycles and purifies existing water
- An iPhone equivalent that can be upgraded without changing all components.

## Example 6: Assistive technology challenge

| Question | How can we create assistive technology products that will support people's independence? |
|---|---|
| Supports content | Technology |
| Stimulus | "Aerodynamically the bumblebee shouldn't be able to fly, but the bumblebee doesn't know that, so it goes on flying anyway" (Mary Kay Ash). |
| | MSFTEnable: "Assistive technology". https://www.youtube.com/watch?v=DBxmADjQlI4 |
| | CIDIaccess: "Independence in your own home with assistive technology". https://www.youtube.com/watch?v=ZceHSARz9zI |
| | Pacercenter: "Assistive technology in action – Meet Elle". https://www.youtube.com/watch?v=g95TO20hnmo |
| Research questions | • What is assistive technology?<br>• Research different types of assistive technology, and the type of people it supports.<br>• What could "support" mean in this context?<br>• Define a target customer that may need assistive technology.<br>• Brainstorm appropriate assistive technology for your product.<br>• Create and refine prototypes. |
| Deliverables | • A prototype of a product that supports your target customer<br>• Details of the design process |
| Microlearning | Video editing |

Some sample outcomes that could be created by this stimulus:
- A watch that supports the person to move, but also keeps track of falls, heart rate and so on
- A home automation system that supports independence.

## Example 7: Virtual reality challenge

| Question | How can virtual reality be used to create fun educational experiences? |
|---|---|
| Supports content | Digital technology, creativity, science, technology, engineering, mathematics |
| Stimulus | "Virtual reality is the first step in a grand adventure into the landscape of the imagination" (Frank Biocca, Taeyong Kim and Mark Levy). <br><br> Science and Literacy: "8 ways how to use virtual reality in the classroom". https://scienceandliteracy.org/how-to-use-virtual-reality-in-the-classroom/ |
| Research questions | • What is virtual reality? <br> • Review how virtual reality is currently being used in education. <br> • Research a concept that you believe could be taught more effectively with virtual reality. <br> • Gain a deep understanding of how the concept works and could be explained. <br> • Brainstorm tasks that might be simplified/improved through the use of virtual reality. |
| Deliverables | • Explanation of design and reasons <br> • Final virtual reality product |
| Microlearning | 3D Worlds – ThingLink introduction |

Some sample outcomes that could be created by this stimulus:
- Learning body systems through VR tour
- Game to test details of planets with VR
- Immersive experience to support understanding of a novel.

## Example 8: Oil spills challenge

| Question | Can we simulate the effects of an oil spill and its subsequent cleanup on all parts of our natural environment? <br><br> How can we use this knowledge to prevent and/or minimise the damage caused by this type of event? |
|---|---|
| Supports content | Sustainability, environment, biology |

| Stimulus | "You simply cannot make more [reefs] unless you have a few thousand years to wait" (Doug Rader). |
| --- | --- |
| | Life Noggin: "What happens after an oil spill?" https://www.youtube.com/watch?v=nshSoLw0tdI |
| Research questions | • How, where, and how often do oil spills occur?<br>• What can be the impact of an oil spill on the natural environment (living and non-living)?<br>• What can be the impact of the cleanup practices on the natural environment (living and non-living)?<br>• Research the terms "skimming" and "disbursement" as they relate to oil spills.<br>• Research oil types – viscosity, volatility, toxicity. |
| Deliverables | • Research regarding the impacts of oil spills on the environment<br>• Presentation showcasing information in whichever format required<br>• Simulated oil spill using vegetable oil on various items – for example, rocks, sand, seashells, feathers (for effects on bird life)<br>• Using appropriate scientific design and referring to your research, focus on which (if any) cleanup techniques work best<br>• Presentation of findings in visual format |
| Microlearning | Video editing |

Some sample outcomes that could be created by this stimulus:

- Examples of ways to prevent the spills
- A concept that binds the oil into a manageable volume.

## Example 9: Smart home challenge

| Question | How can we create a product or process that uses smart home technology to meet the needs of homeowners? |
| --- | --- |
| Supports content | Technology, electronics, internet of things |
| Stimulus | "Design is not what it looks like and feels like, design is how it works" (Steve Jobs). |
| | "It's not that we use technology, it's that we live technology" (Godfrey Reggio). |
| | Eye on Tech: "What is a smart home or smart building?" https://www.youtube.com/watch?v=IC0mkHh7MaA |
| | EconocomTV: "Internet of things". https://www.youtube.com/watch?v=p_R5ZVWMhzM |

| | |
|---|---|
| Research questions | • What is a smart home and smart technology?<br>• What is the internet of things?<br>• Research examples in Australian homes.<br>• What are some advantages and disadvantages of smart technology?<br>• Create a target customer, and research how smart technology might support the customer.<br>• Is there a smart technology item that you could create that would be useful for your target customer and does not already exist?<br>• How could you expand variations of this product to support other customers? |
| Deliverables | • A prototype of a smart technology product that supports the life of your target customer<br>• Video or poster showcasing the product |
| Microlearning | • Video editing<br>• Microbit introduction<br>• Design introduction<br>• Prototype design |

Solutions that could be presented by this challenge:

- Preventing elderly falls, calling ambulances
- Security for pets, feeding and talking when absent.

## Example 10: Cryptography challenge

| Question | Can we develop our cryptography skills to create a puzzle-based challenge for others? |
|---|---|
| Supports content | Cryptography, computational thinking, creativity, critical thinking |
| Stimulus | "When cryptography is outlawed, bayl bhgynjf jvyy unir cevinpl" (John Perry Barlow).<br><br>"It is possible to invent a single machine which can be used to compute any computable sequence" (Alan Turing).<br><br>Khan Academy: "What is cryptography?"<br>https://www.khanacademy.org/computing/computer-science/cryptography/crypt/v/intro-to-cryptography |

| | |
|---|---|
| **Research questions** | • What is cryptography?<br>• How has cryptography been used in the last 100 years?<br>• What are some different types of cryptography?<br>• Research definitions of code-breaking and ciphers.<br>• Research different types of ciphers and test yourself with the ciphers your teacher has provided.<br>• Create a target customer that would enjoy your code-breaking challenge.<br>• Design your own ciphers/codes.<br>• These can be developed into a challenge such as:<br>  – A scavenger hunt<br>  – An escape room<br>• Your solution can be in printed or electronic form. |
| **Deliverables** | • A prototype of your code-breaking challenge<br>• A poster or document discussion containing types of code-breaking that were employed in your challenge<br>• Solutions to your challenge!! |
| **Microlearning** | 3D Worlds – ThingLink introduction |

Solutions that could be presented by this challenge:
- Binary puzzle
- Group scavenger hunt challenge.

## Example 11: Urban infrastructure challenge

| | |
|---|---|
| **Question** | How can we restore and maintain urban infrastructure? |
| **Supports content** | Global understanding of living environments; sustainability, health and wellbeing of culture and community |
| **Stimulus** | "Show me a healthy community with a healthy economy and I will show you a community that has its green infrastructure in order and understands the relationship between the built and the unbuilt environment" (Will Rogers).<br><br>"A successful society is characterised by a rising living standard for its population" (Robert Trout).<br><br>World Economic Forum: "Infrastructure and urban development". https://www.youtube.com/watch?v=kNvmaq3e3Hk<br><br>CNBC Explains: "What is a smart city?" https://www.youtube.com/watch?v=bANfnYDTzxE<br><br>LinkedIn Learning: "Smart cities: Solving urban problems using technology". https://www.youtube.com/watch?v=nnyRZotnPSU |

| Research questions | - What is urban infrastructure, and which parts of our community does it relate to?
- Why is good infrastructure important for local, national, and international communities?
- Research examples of urban infrastructure solutions.
- Describe a target customer that could be supported by an improvement in urban infrastructure. |
|---|---|
| Deliverables | - A prototype of a product that improves urban infrastructure for the target customer
- Details explaining design process |
| Microlearning | - Video editing
- Microbit introduction
- Microbit extension |

Solutions that could be presented by this challenge:

- Bee colonies and solar-panelled integrated roofing
- Wind turbines in the middle of highways to create power.

CHAPTER 13

# Microlearning content

One of the key components for success in STEAM education is the effectiveness of your learning resources. YouTube videos are great for your own learning, but are often long-winded and may contain unnecessary details or inappropriate content or language. The maximum video length for optimum student attention is less than five minutes, but around three minutes is preferable.

So, we need to find another, more efficient way to give students and educators what they need in a concise, easy-to-manage format. This comes in the form of microlearnings.

> For about 15 years, I have used microlearnings, well before I knew there was a name for this type of educational tool. The process for me started when trying to deal with students who needed repetition after face-to-face learning. This then morphed into creating short instruction sets for students who needed extension. It allowed students to work exactly where they needed within their learning experience without it being obvious that they were doing work that was repetition or extension.
>
> I then realised the benefit for time-poor educators who had to learn what they needed quickly and concisely. Two years ago, I learnt that there is a name for what I have been doing and I have since embraced this type of learning within the Authentic STEAM Framework.

## What is microlearning?

The definitions vary, but basically it is short and focused learning that allows students to view and focus on content that is directly related to their needs. A similar, older term is "just-in-time" learning.

These learnings have long been part of my educational practice and work well with my hybrid personalised approach to digital technology learning. The hybrid approach is a combination of face-to-face, printed, and online components, which allows all students to thrive, independent of ability and experience.

As far as the Authentic STEAM Framework is concerned, this approach is essential, as it allows students to focus on pockets of learning they are unsure of or need to revisit. It also allows them to skip any learnings that are not required because the knowledge has already been gained or an alternative has been used.

The idea behind the microlearnings is that they are used when needed. If students have completed similar tasks before, they may not need to use them. Microlearnings are also there to support educators in learning the components that are required for completing the tasks.

## Types of microlearning

Generally, microlearning takes the form of video, audio, picture or text, as these are the most accessible and easy-to-produce formats. Videos are seen as an effective form of communication, as they can be viewed on many different delivery devices. Ghafar & Abdullkarim (2023) discuss the need to explore other types of microlearnings: "eLearning, video games, blogs, podcasts, infographics, and different types of visual content are a few more examples. The next step is to choose the media most suitable for the circumstance and the educational requirements".

This final point is the most important component of the microlearning experience. Microlearnings are highly effective when used appropriately to enhance teaching and learning. Mapping the resource to the students' needs and the learning experience is essential.

## Advantages of using microlearning

Microlearning offers several advantages for both teachers and students. Some of the key benefits are discussed below.

## Advantages for teachers

- **Flexibility of planning.** Microlearning allows educators to accommodate diverse learners and encourage students to pursue areas of interest and challenge.
- **Personalised learning.** They allow for a more personalised approach, catering for individual needs and requirements for teaching and learning strategies.
- **Brief and focused.** Learning in short and sharp bursts, with highly focused responses to a learning need, means that the updating, revision and presentation of information can be completed quickly. The need for students to focus for extended lengths of time is reduced. In the world of easily accessible and on-demand content, students' attention spans may suffer, and "making a strategy to give students enough engaging material that is simple to grasp is one method to solve this difficulty" (Ghafar & Abdullkarim, 2023).
- **Assessment feedback.** By integrating small and focused assessments into microlearning modules, an assessment of student understanding can be achieved quickly. Students will receive feedback while the learning is still fresh in their mind.
- **Engagement.** Quick and focused learning is more likely to engage and maintain student attention, leading to students being more engaged and less overwhelmed.

## Advantages for students

- **Reinforcement and speed.** Microlearning allows students to engage with content at their own speed and in their own time. If the microlearnings are presented in a written or video format, students will be able to revisit learning to reinforce their learning or deepen their understanding.
- **Improved retention.** It is much easier to learn for the long-term attainment of information and knowledge if the content is presented in smaller, manageable chunks, particularly if students are then using that learning within a short space of time.
- **Cater to students' own diverse learning requirements.** Because of the way that microlearning can be presented, it allows students to access the learning they need when they need it, in the way that they need it.

- **Self-directed.** Students (and educators) can use microlearning resources to extend or reinforce learning at their own pace, and to follow paths of interest.
- **Used in various teaching formats.** Microlearnings can support students when needed, in face-to-face, online or hybrid (mixture of face-to-face and online) formats.
- **Reducing cognitive load.** Cognitive load is the amount of information that the working memory can hold at any one time, and varies between students. In their research, Susilana et al. (2022) found that producing and providing microlearnings "is useful for easing students' intrinsic, ancillary, and relevant cognitive loads during online learning". This is also true for educators, as producing microlearnings can mean smaller coursework produced rapidly over time.

These are all wonderful reasons to use microlearnings in your classroom. Your classroom will function and work more efficiently. Students who need extending can be extended, and those who need further support can access it easily.

These microlearnings can take time to produce, but if created a step at a time, individual resources will turn into a large bank of resources that can be used time and time again.

## How to use microlearnings as part of your pedagogical approach

There are two main approaches to using microlearning within your classroom. They are "just-in-time" teaching and "flipped learning". These concepts are shown in further detail below.

### *Just-in-time teaching*

This concept is not new to educators. It is a method that has been used by educators for decades and has proven to be very effective, though it is not always paired with digital technology. In essence, it is the practice of educators giving students what they need, at the time that they need it, in the way that they need it.

The newer difference in the process is using microlearning to enhance, consolidate or develop understanding of content requirements. As a student needs content, the content is available to them on demand, through learning management systems, content development sites, and web-builders.

The key to the success of this format is that the required microlearning is available at the time that the student needs it, so that there is no delay between when the learning is required and when it is produced. The added advantage of having microlearnings pre-recorded or pre-written is that different students with different educational requirements can access learning at different times.

### *Flipped learning*

Flipped learning has been around for a long time but has had a renaissance of late. In the past, it was seen as a method for students to improve their knowledge through "face-to-face interaction in the classroom with independent study outside of it, often through viewing assigned video content" (Nazdan, 2018).

While this format has been shown to improve student outcomes (Nazdan, 2018), the longer videos are not as engaging for today's students. There is also the issue of students' access to large files effectively depending on their internet or computer access at home, contributing to the division of students into those who can and cannot access technology in their home or school environment. This is known as the "digital divide".

The more contemporary way to use the flipped learning approach is to create shorter and sharper microlearnings for students. These videos or other content are then made available to the students in a format that is accessible to them. This content is then suggested as an enhancement to existing learning, but is rarely made compulsory as homework, thus helping to reduce students' workload outside the classroom.

## Authentic STEAM microlearning

Below are instructions for some of the key options that are required within the Authentic STEAM Framework. The software described here has been chosen because it is freely available via the internet or on a basic PC. This software can be substituted by other options, but these microlearnings have all been used successfully within the framework. Videos related to these microlearnings can be accessed free of charge at STEAMauthenticity.com.

## Getting started microlearning

This focuses on the basic understanding of the task students are about to work on. The idea is to give an overview, then starting points. This is a short video of less than one minute.

## Target customer

Target customers are an essential component of the Authentic STEAM Framework, and in design thinking in general. A target customer is an individual that is most likely to buy your product.

You will need to focus on designing your target customer. Think about their age and needs and what they do and do not want from their products.

Give the person a name, a gender, clothing, a job, and so on, as this will make you feel like you are creating a product for a real person. Draw an image of that person that you can refer to.

## Beginning design

This microlearning focuses on the first three components of the Authentic STEAM Framework.

It describes how this will fit into your problem-solving challenge. It focuses on what makes good design, and how to begin the brainstorming process.

## Further design

This microlearning focuses on the final two components of the Authentic STEAM Framework.

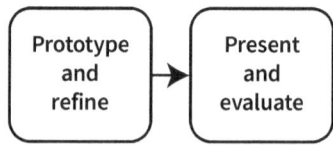

Its primary intention is to look at completing the development and refinement of the design process. This is specified in a simplified way in this process, then detailed later in the other microlearnings.

### *Prototyping and variations*

This microlearning focuses on what prototyping is and how to go about creating samples and variations. It gives examples and shows how to break the process down into manageable steps.

### *Presentation*

This microlearning is about what makes a good presentation, and how to be concise and make it appealing to others so they can understand how the process of creating a sales pitch would work.

### *Evaluation*

This covers concepts that allow students to achieve to the best of their ability through peer- and self-assessment.

## Software microlearnings

The microlearnings for the software packages that match with the challenge tasks are essential to the effective use of the Authentic STEAM Framework. All the text-based versions of the instructions can be found in **Part 5: Microlearnings and skill development**.

The content is separated into:

- Algorithm and structure
- Coding
- Virtual and augmented reality
- General skills.

# PART 4
# THE SIMPLIFIED STEAM FRAMEWORK

"The beautiful thing about learning is that no one can take it away from you."

– B. B. KING

CHAPTER 14

# The Simplified STEAM Framework

The Authentic STEAM Framework focuses on the development of critical, design and computational skills. It allows students to gain confidence while focusing on open-ended, project-based learning tasks. However, there is often the need for a simplified framework that could work well for simpler consolidation tasks.

The simplified tasks shown in the Simplified STEAM Framework are also useful as a way for an educator to initially dip their toe into design thinking. This can be through various formats:

- Short case studies, where the concepts and possible solutions are still open-ended, but some of the basic information is provided, meaning that less research is required
- Problem-solving challenges which involve design thinking.

The bridge between the two formats is the need to use an iterative process to develop solutions, and the ability to have multiple correct solutions to the challenges put in front of the students.

The structure for the Simplified STEAM Framework is the same as that of the Authentic STEAM Framework, but with simplified categories, and is ideal for tasks to be completed in a shorter timeframe. The basic simplified framework is shown below:

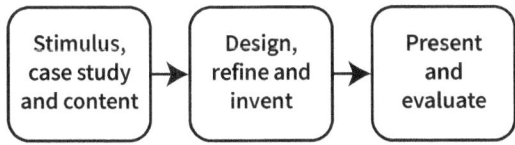

## Sample Template – Simplified STEAM Framework

| | |
|---|---|
| Stimulus, case study and content | |
| Design, refine and invent | |
| Present and evaluate | |

## Example 1: Plywood chair design (design technology)

| | |
|---|---|
| Stimulus, case study and content | How can we design simple furniture made from accessible resources that can be dismantled and reassembled easily?<br><br>Stan is a recent tiny home buyer who lives in a tiny home. He wants to create a design for a modular outdoor chair that can be broken down and stored when not in use. If possible, he would like to find a way that uses most of the plywood sheets with minimal waste. Stan wants to create something that is stylish. He would like you to design him either two chairs, or a chair and side table. It will need to fit on one piece of plywood of size 2400 mm x 1200 mm. |
| Design, refine and invent | 1. Questions to consider:<br>• What makes a good chair design?<br>• Will the chair hold Stan and his visitors?<br>• How easy will it be to put together and pull apart?<br>2. Create at least four sample designs.<br>• Each chair will need to come from one sheet of plywood.<br>• Use the questions you considered in the previous section. |
| Present and evaluate | 1. Create a smaller sample chair or chairs using cardboard cut to 240 mm x 120 mm.<br>2. Create a poster or short video that shows the benefits of the chair and the design features you have used.<br>3. Discuss:<br>• What went well with designing this project?<br>• How could you make the design process simpler next time?<br>• What other products would be useful for Stan that are either collapsible or have dual purpose? |

# Example 2: Junkyard cars (design technology and science laws of motion)

| Stimulus, case study and content | How can we design a small car out of waste materials that will travel the fastest or farthest on a kinetic ramp?<br><br>You will compete in a challenge to get a car with no motor or propulsion to move as far along the gravity-fed track as possible. You will need to use recycled or found objects to create your car. Your car must fit the dimensions of the track:<br><br>• Maximum width: 75 mm<br>• Minimum distance between the inside of the wheels: 37 mm<br>• Minimum height of the belly of the car: 7mm<br><br>Ideas and examples can be found at https://nerdyderby.com/#main |
|---|---|
| Design, refine and invent | 1. Questions to consider:<br><br>• What do we need to understand about the laws of motion?<br>• What do we need to understand about the shape and weight of the car?<br>• What do we need to understand about wheels and axles?<br><br>2. Draw at least four sample designs before building.<br><br>• Once you have created your designs, create prototypes and test variations with one change at a time to enable you to find which is fastest.<br>• Race your cars against others to find the best car. "Best" could be either speed or distance (or both). |
| Present and evaluate | 1. Create a poster that contains:<br><br>• An image of your final design, with details labelled<br>• A copy of your designs leading up to the final choice<br><br>2. Discuss:<br><br>• What changes did you need to make to get the car to go farther/faster?<br>• What issues came up during the car design process?<br>• What would you explain to others about your design choices? |

# Example 3: Kinetic sculpture (design technology, laws of motion)

| | |
|---|---|
| **Stimulus, case study and content** | How can we design and build a sculpture that is beautiful but also uses kinetic energy to move?<br><br>Blick Art Materials: "Kinetic sculpture". https://www.youtube.com/watch?v=qs88aC0k0yI<br><br>Ross McSweeney: "Kinetic wave automata". https://www.etsy.com/au/listing/1466791257/kinetic-wave-automata-moving-sculpture<br><br>Research some simple kinetic designs using various stimuli and look for simple concepts that could be produced easily. |
| **Design, refine and invent** | 1. Questions to consider:<br>- What can we find out about kinetic energy?<br>- How can we design some simple shapes for the laser cutter that will allow us to build our design?<br><br>2. Design various kinetic examples of your own, keeping in mind:<br>- How it looks and moves<br>- The movements you would like to see your model make<br>- How easy it will be to create your model |
| **Present and evaluate** | 1. Present your designs<br>2. Present your final model in person-to-person or video format<br>3. Discuss:<br>- What did you learn about creating kinetic sculptures?<br>- How would you change/improve your design if you were completing it again?<br>- Can you think of another way that the skills you have learnt could be translated to a different challenge? |

# Example 4: Beautiful and useful garden design

| Stimulus, case study and content | How can we reimagine an item for a garden that is useful and improves the functionality of the space?<br><br>You have been asked to design something that will enhance the functionality of a garden space, but will also add to the beauty of the space. You may create a product that is either multipurpose or has a definite function but is sculptural or beautiful within the space.<br><br>The garden item is to be designed for a keen gardener who has a very functional garden but is looking for something that they would find visually pleasing as they reach retirement age. |
|---|---|
| Design, refine and invent | 1. Questions to consider:<br>• What are some useful products for a garden?<br>• What are beautiful elements that can be found within a garden?<br>• How could something that is useful become beautiful?<br>• How could something that is beautiful become useful?<br><br>2. Research and create using printed or online tools.<br>• Design a variety of products.<br>• Select a product that would most suit your client. You are free to use whichever raw material suits your design.<br><br>3. Create many variations of your chosen product, then settle on a design that would suit your client best.<br><br>4. Create a sample of the product. |
| Present and evaluate | 1. Build your project for a target customer, so that it meets their wants or needs in their ideal garden environment.<br><br>2. Prepare a presentation in a format of your choice to showcase each of your garden design variations.<br><br>3. Add to the presentation your final design suggestions.<br><br>4. Discuss:<br>• What went well with the project?<br>• What issues did you have in the design process?<br>• How did you solve the issues?<br>• What could you do better next time? |

# Example 5: AI facial recognition material design (digital and design technology)

| Stimulus, case study and content | A clothing company based in Turin has created fabric that confuses facial recognition software and make it difficult for a person to be identified. Your role is to research this and design a fabric that will create the same effect. |
|---|---|
| | Loz Blain: "Flamboyant Italian clothes defeat facial recognition without masks." https://newatlas.com/good-thinking/facial-recognition-clothes/ |
| | Dan Mekinec: "The benefits of face recognition technology." https://visagetechnologies.com/benefits-of-face-recognition/ |
| Design, refine and invent | 1. Questions to consider:<br>• What is facial recognition software used for? What are the pros and cons?<br>• How does that patterning of the fabric confuse the artificial intelligence facial recognition?<br>• What components would make a good design for such a fabric?<br>• What makes a good design for fabric so that people would want to wear it?<br>• How could we ensure that we have provided the correct components to reduce the chances of facial recognition? |
| | 2. Research and create using printed or online tools. Create individual sections that can be tessellated (repeated). Vary colours and designs until you have at least four options. |
| | "Online personalised digital fabric design web-to-print software." https://www.designnbuy.com/digital-textile-printing-software.html |
| | 3. Use collage or your computer to show how your fabric could be showcased. |
| | 4. Name each design appropriately. |
| Present and evaluate | 1. Prepare a presentation in a format of your choice to showcase each of your named fabric options.<br>2. Add to the presentation your final wearable design suggestions.<br>3. Discuss:<br>• What was something interesting you learnt during the research process?<br>• Why did you decide on your final design?<br>• What were some issues you discovered in the design process?<br>• What could you do differently next time? |

# Example 6: Fast fashion (design technology and sustainability)

| | |
|---|---|
| **Stimulus, case study and content** | Every year 92 million tonnes of fabric waste are placed in landfill.<br><br>Earth.Org: "10 concerning fast fashion waste statistics." https://earth.org/statistics-about-fast-fashion-waste/<br><br>Your task is to find ways to reduce this amount by creating a fashion item from pre-loved clothing. This item can be an item of clothing, but you may like to think laterally to come up with something else fashion-related. |
| **Design, refine and invent** | 1. Questions to consider:<br>• What are the issues with clothing ending in landfill?<br>• Is there a particular area of the fashion community that is causing the most landfill?<br>• What efforts have been made to reduce landfill?<br>• What products would work best in upcycling or reimagining fashion items?<br><br>2. Immerse yourself in the options through an existing wardrobe or visiting your local op shop to find suitable items.<br><br>3. Draw and invent at least five different designs for your upcycled fashion item.<br><br>4. Decide on your best design and use the recycled clothing to complete your design. |
| **Present and evaluate** | 1. Create a presentation that will:<br>• Discuss your design choices in detail<br>• Show your design variations<br>• Showcase images of initial designs and the final product<br><br>2. Discuss:<br>• What went well with the project?<br>• What did not go so well?<br>• How did you solve the issues?<br>• What could you do better next time? |

# Example 7: Gender-neutral uniform design (design tech – textiles)

| Stimulus, case study and content | How can we create a unique range of uniform pieces that meet the needs of a school? |
|---|---|
| | Many businesses that require staff to wear uniforms are now producing products that promote comfort and choice, as well as not conforming to gender stereotypes. School uniform is generally an exception to that, being gender-specific and often lacking comfort and appropriate responses to activities and weather. Your task is to design uniform options that meet the needs of both genders, and each piece needs to have the ability to be worn by either gender. |
| Design, refine and invent | 1. Questions to consider:<br>• What age group are you focusing your designs on?<br>• What would a typical student of that age need from a uniform?<br>• How could the school colours and spirit be represented in your design?<br>• How could all the uniform options work together as a whole?<br><br>2. Design on paper or electronically at least six separate items that would work together as a cohesive set. The uniform should work for school colours, both genders, different seasons and movement. |
| Present and evaluate | 1. Create a presentation that includes:<br>• Which age group are you designing for?<br>• What are the needs of your chosen age group?<br>• Fabric and colour samples<br>• Designs and how they work together<br><br>2. Discuss:<br>• What were some issues that were discovered in the design process?<br>• How did you solve the issues?<br>• What would you change next time? |

# Example 8: Smart clothing

| Stimulus, case study and content | How can we create a smart clothing item that will support health and wellbeing? |
|---|---|
| | Your challenge is to focus on how you might create a smart clothing product. This might include ideas such as: |
| | • A hat that keeps an eye on your UV exposure or changes that exposure as heat increases<br>• Body temperature and dehydration<br>• Workout or game day wearables that focus on heart rate and distance travelled |
| | Before beginning, focus on your target customer, give them a name, age, circumstances, and a need for smart clothing. Ask yourself, "Who needs my smart clothing?" Is it an elite sports person, or an elderly person, or someone somewhere in between. |
| | Mark Donnison: "E-textiles and wearables tutorials & resources." https://kitronik.co.uk/blogs/resources/e-textiles-wearables-tutorials-resources |
| | Karen Butler: "Wearable tech." https://www.youtube.com/playlist?list=PLF5HEj4xFkVGcjYUr_iNfRbpxKn-jacFL |
| Design, refine and invent | Questions to consider:<br><br>• What is "smart clothing" and what are some of the ways that it can be utilised?<br>• Design your "smart clothing" item or items, showing your design process and reasoning behind your choices. Create your prototypes in colour variations.<br>• Once you have decided on your design, look at the microlearnings that are available.<br>• Code the Microbit you have been allocated to meet the needs of your clothing. |
| Present and evaluate | 1. Create a sample of your smart clothing<br>2. Develop a presentation that will show:<br><br>• Your final design, including its features and benefits<br>• Your Microbit design and coding<br>• A video or real-life demonstration of how your smart clothing option works |
| | **Teacher note:** This task will require some pre-preparation on both the student's and educator's part. Some of the microlearnings available in Chapter 17 show Microbit coding that supports the process. This is a great way to create a cross-curricular task. |

## Example 9: Protecting native wildlife (science, environmental)

| | |
|---|---|
| **Stimulus, case study and content** | How can we create a product or process that will support and protect our native wildlife?<br><br>You have been asked by a local wildlife protection group to research and develop ways that will support and protect our native wildlife. |
| **Design, refine and invent** | 1. Questions to consider:<br><br>• Which parts of our native wildlife are in danger?<br>• What are the biggest dangers to our wildlife?<br>• Who could we talk to that could help us understand what is needed?<br>• What has already been created to support wildlife conservation?<br><br>2. Design and brainstorm some options for your product or process.<br><br>3. Refine your ideas down to one idea.<br><br>4. Create a prototype or mock-up to support your idea. |
| **Present and evaluate** | 1. Develop your prototype<br><br>2. Develop a presentation that will show:<br><br>• What your final design is, and what its features and benefits are |

## Example 10: Rock, paper, scissors game

| | |
|---|---|
| **Stimulus, case study and content** | You have been asked to create a game using algorithm design and coding to build the game. |
| **Design, refine and invent** | 1. Questions to consider:<br><br>• What are the basic components of a rock, paper, scissors game?<br>• How can the game be broken down into manageable steps?<br>• How can those manageable steps then be coded?<br><br>2. Create a data flow diagram to show how these steps work together.<br><br>3. Begin at the simplest part (getting images or words for the rock, paper and scissors to appear on the screen) then build from there.<br><br>4. Remember to test as you go.<br><br>**Teacher note:** The final product is less important than the conversations along the way and the development of problem-solving ability. |

| Present and evaluate | 1. Create a journal detailing problems, successes, and thoughts about the coding process. |
| --- | --- |
| | 2. Final product. |
| | **Teacher note:** While the product has not been described here, this could be created in Scratch, Microbits, Python and so on. These are listed in order of difficulty. Once again, the process is what is important, not the final product. |

## Example 11: Cyber safety challenge (digital technology and creative)

| Stimulus, case study and content | You have been asked by your school to develop a program or educational product that will support the younger students at your school to be safe when they are online. You will need to produce this in such a way that it is easy to understand but does not talk down to them. |
| --- | --- |
| Design, refine and invent | 1. Questions to consider:<br>• Which age group are you developing this program for?<br>• What is cyber safety?<br>• What are the biggest issues surrounding cyber safety for that age group?<br>2. Define the key issue or issues you would like to focus on.<br>3. Brainstorm the best way to communicate this information to the age group you are interested in.<br>4. Create the content on cyber safety you wish to present.<br>5. Present in a way that will be visually engaging (e.g. video, animation, comic, short story). |
| Present and evaluate | Present your final product, with explanations as to why choices were made.<br>**Teacher note:** While this task is for a younger group, it is a great way for students to understand the issues surrounding cyber safety. |

## Example 12: Bioplastic research (biology and chemistry)

| Stimulus, case study and content | You have been asked to research existing plastics and how we use them, then create bioplastics and test their durability and ability to break down. |
| --- | --- |
| | Hyundai Motorstudio: "5 ways to make bioplastic easily and quickly." https://hyundai.motorstudio.co.id/senayan-park/newsrooms/how-to-make-bioplastic |

| Design, refine and invent | 1. Questions to consider:<br>• Look at three or more general household products that use plastic for packaging.<br>• Research how well these products break down in our environment.<br>• Research other alternatives, including bioplastics.<br>2. Part 1: Design alternative packaging for these three products, describing why changes have been made and what the benefits are.<br>3. Part 2: Create bioplastics samples.<br>4. Once created, design a scientific experiment that will test the effectiveness of each of the bioplastics. |
|---|---|
| Present and evaluate | Create a presentation that will:<br>• Identify your original products and your alternative packaging designs<br>• Showcase your experiment design<br>• Show results in table form<br>• Include observations and conclusions. |

## Example 13: The importance of soil quality (biology and chemistry)

| Stimulus, case study and content | How does soil quality affect plant growth?<br>You will need to design an experiment that will allow you to develop an understanding about which additives to soil can either reduce or improve plant growth. |
|---|---|
| Design, refine and invent | 1. Questions to consider:<br>• What types of soil can successfully grow plants?<br>• Which soils are unable to successfully grow plants?<br>• Select one soil variation to test (salt, sand, pollution of some kind)<br>2. Part 1: Design an experiment that will test your soil variation, describing how this will be able to test the effectiveness of the product either to help or hinder growth of the plant.<br>3. Part 2: Complete your experiment with the product provided. |
| Present and evaluate | Create a presentation that will:<br>• Identify your research surrounding plant growth.<br>• Showcase your experiment design.<br>• Show results in table form.<br>• Include observations and conclusions. |

CHAPTER 15

# The Primary-based STEAM Framework

The focus of this framework is to establish a specific STEAM approach for primary school users. Challenges are shorter and simpler, but still require some focus on target customers and defining for a particular person or situation. The term "target customer" will not necessarily be used, but the concept will be introduced at this earlier stage.

This framework also works on the development of student agency and understanding the importance of an iterative process for the development of concepts.

In their research, Voicu et al. (2023) state that primary teachers feel the need for "more specialised training on STEAM, for a deeper understanding of the STEAM philosophy, ideas, methods, and the need for more teaching resources (preferably digital) such as lesson plans and educational materials". Using the Simplified STEAM Framework shown here should provide a strong starting point for primary educators to begin their successful journey within STEAM.

The example challenges shown below could be used within student workstations for students to research and reach multiple solutions. This would enhance the iterative process and allow students to develop their creative and design thinking.

As you will see later in this chapter, the Primary-based STEAM Framework maps directly to the other frameworks – the Simplified STEAM and Authentic STEAM Frameworks. They should be seen as stepping stones from one to another – a building of skills to establish intrinsically motivated, creative thinkers.

## Sample template

| Challenge name | |
|---|---|
| What is our challenge? | |
| How can we find out about it? | |
| How can we design a solution? | |
| What can we create? | |
| How can we show our learning? | |

Each of these challenges is quite simple from a design perspective. The key requirement is that there needs to be some student agency in how the challenges are carried out. A common theme seen during research for this book was that students are often given a very definite way to build and research.

Essential to a successful STEAM inquiry process is:
- Engagement in a design process
- The capacity to use creativity and develop creative thinking
- The ability to create iterations and interpretations for the final product
- The ability to express findings in various ways.

The positioning of these challenges is open to interpretation. Sometimes they can be completed as an addition to class studies, but often flipping that dynamic can be useful.

In a primary school environment, creating several challenges within a classroom, then allowing students to explore and develop their own skills and understanding can be effective. There should also be an understanding that some students come with existing understanding, experience and knowledge.

Discussion, scope for creativity, and the development of computational and strategic thinking skills are essential to the success of STEAM tasks and programs.

An effective strategy for pre-discussion with your students focuses on three questions:

- What do you already know?
- What would you like to know?
- How can we find out?

Doing this anonymously through an electronic pinboard is a very effective way to gather responses. Alternatively, a short electronic survey where students can answer/ask questions around these pre-discussion guidelines is also effective. Students who may not participate in a face-to-face class discussion may be more comfortable to do so in one of these formats.

Within a primary school environment, it is often useful to add guiding questions to help students focus on learning. Li et al., (2022) discussed that "by adding guiding questions on the scaffolding, students could direct their thinking and analyse the problems more deeply." They went on further to say that this practice contains its own risk, as it may inhibit the ability of the student to think independently and effectively. The balance between these options is best worked out through trial and error, and may differ from student to student and class to class.

Li et al. (2022) go on to discuss the need for a consistent and dedicated approach to teaching STEAM, rather than an ad hoc format, with particular focus on "integrating STEAM education into the formal curriculum and putting it into the curriculum schedule together with general subject courses". This allows STEAM capabilities to be embedded into the general classroom structure.

# Example 1: Adaption (middle to upper primary)

| Challenge name | Adapting to life |
|---|---|
| What is our challenge? | To understand how living things (plants and animals) adapt to their environment |
| How can we find out about it? | Questions to consider:<br>• What is adaption?<br>• Why do animals and plants adapt to their environments?<br>• What are selection pressures, and what are some examples where a species has changed to suit a new environment?<br><br>Select an animal or plant and research how its characteristics ensure survival in its environment. |
| How can we design a solution? | 1. Take an existing species and decide on a real or imagined pressure on the species. Examples might be:<br>• Climate change<br>• Loss of habitat<br>• Separation through natural disaster<br><br>2. Design changes that might happen to the species because of this change in environment. |
| What can we create? | A poster or similar showcasing:<br>• The original animal or plant<br>• What the change in environment is<br>• What the resulting change in the animal or plant will be |
| How can we show our learning? | • Visual representation of adaption<br>• Completion of simple details or a conversation to show depth of understanding. |

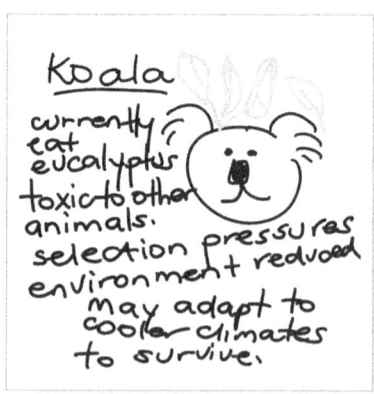

# Example 2: Making mobiles (middle to upper primary)

| Challenge name | Making mobiles |
|---|---|
| What is our challenge? | To create a mobile of at least four levels. It must be made from the skewers/dowels, string, aluminium foil and Plasticine provided for you. The key is to balance the mobile so that the skewers are completely horizontal. The connections between layers should not be through the centre of the skewer/dowel. |
| How can we find out about it? | Questions to consider:<br>• What makes a good hanging mobile?<br>• What do we need to understand about how items balance?<br>• How can we make the skewers or dowels sit horizontally? |
| How can we design a solution? | 1. Draw the initial design on paper, and discuss how what you have learnt through research is represented.<br>2. Experiment with balancing hanging items from skewers/dowels (a place to hang is essential to this – a portable clothes rack or hooks under a shelf work well).<br>3. Through trial and error, find a solution to creating an effective hanging mobile. |
| What can we create? | • A four-level hanging mobile<br>• Details of iterations and drawings |
| How can we show our learning? | • The final product<br>• Details in a journal or poster showing thinking and development of understanding. |

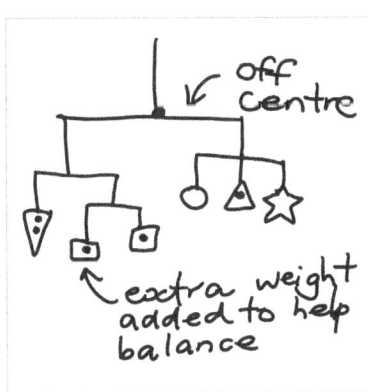

# Example 3: Designer insects (lower to middle primary)

| Challenge name | Designer insects |
|---|---|
| What is our challenge? | To create a unique insect using the elements provided for you. Despite being unique, the insect must have all the elements of a true insect. |
| How can we find out about it? | Research identifiable parts of a bug. For example: legs, antennae, body parts.<br><br>Insect Identification: "BugFinder: Insect search/identification tool." https://www.insectidentification.org/bugfinder-start.php |
| How can we design a solution? | 1. Design at least four variations of your insect before deciding on your final choice.<br>2. Label the parts of the insect to show your understanding. |
| What can we create? | • Create a 3D model of your insect and name it and label the parts. |
| How can we show our learning? | • Show your decisions around why this is the perfect designer insect.<br>• Compare your insect to others in the class and work together on a classification structure to show how the insects might be grouped together. |

# Example 4: Friction marble run (middle to upper primary)

| Challenge name | Friction marble run |
|---|---|
| What is our challenge? | Create a marble run using marble run blocks or tubing. The trick is to use friction so that the marble run takes a specific amount of time (e.g. 16 seconds). |
| How can we find out about it? | Questions to consider:<br>• How does friction work?<br>• What items might slow something down?<br>• What items might make something go faster? |
| How can we design a solution? | Test many different items and combinations of products to get your marble run to work for exactly 16 seconds (or whatever time has been chosen). |
| What can we create? | Complete and test your marble run. Objects can be used such as:<br>• Velcro<br>• Plasticine or Play-Doh<br>• Vaseline<br>• Angles and obstacles |
| How can we show our learning? | • Create a poster that shows your design thinking.<br>• Video or demonstrate your marble run for your teacher. |

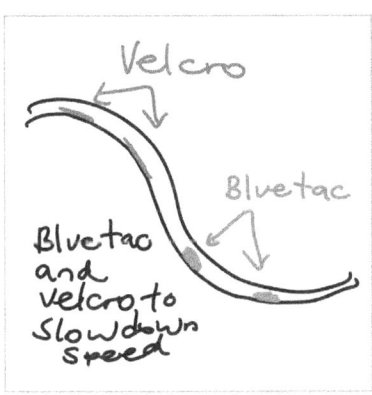

# Example 5: Centre of gravity (middle to upper primary)

| Challenge name | Centre of gravity |
|---|---|
| What is our challenge? | To understand what "centre of gravity" is, how it can change for different objects, and how it can be applied in real-life scenarios. |
| How can we find out about it? | Questions to consider:<br>• What is "centre of gravity"?<br>• What real-life situations can it affect?<br>• What sort of items or situations have you seen that are affected by centre of gravity? |
| How can we design a solution? | 1. Create several different shapes.<br>2. Insert a push pin in a pin board from which will hang a string and a weight (making a plumb line).<br>3. Pin each shape to the pin board from at least five different positions.<br>4. Draw the line shown by the plumb line.<br>5. Repeat for each shape.<br>6. Develop an understanding of what you have seen during the process.<br>7. Try more complex shapes such as those shown below and continue to experiment. |
| What can we create? | • How can we develop what we have learnt into real-life situations?<br>• What do the plumb lines on the shapes tell us? |
| How can we show our learning? | • What do you notice?<br>• What have we learnt about centre of gravity?<br>• Present your findings to your teacher/class to develop understanding.<br>• How can what you have learnt apply to real life? |

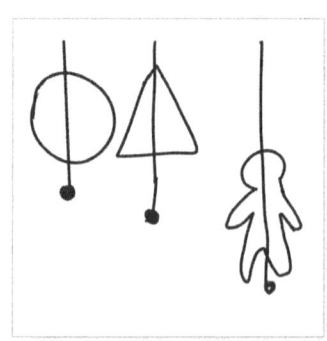

# Example 6: Stop and go challenge. Can you be a robot?

| Challenge name | Stop and go (early childhood) |
|---|---|
| What is our challenge? | To follow directions EXACTLY as they are given to us. Directions could be:<br>• Left<br>• Forward<br>• Sit<br>• Right<br>• Backward<br>• Stand<br><br>A fully completed example is shown below. |
| How can we find out about it? | The teacher will need to create cards – laminated would work best – with the number of steps written in whiteboard pen.<br>• Initially teacher-led.<br>• Place four or five cards to start in the order that they should be completed.<br>• Complete simple algorithms, and practise with the class.<br>• Make a mistake in one instruction while teaching so that students understand that the instructions need to be in order. |
| How can we design a solution? | Once students understand the concepts, get them to work in pairs or small groups to develop algorithms (instructions to follow). |
| What can we create? | • Get students to add their own instructions – e.g. hop three times – and create more and more detailed algorithms.<br>• Students can only move in the direction they are facing, so will need to move LEFT or RIGHT if needed.<br>• Depending on age, you could put an IF statement in – e.g. IF have blue eyes go LEFT 1 step, else go RIGHT one step. |
| How can we show our learning? | Through group work and showing understanding through creating and working with choices. |

| START |
|---|
| FORWARD 3 steps |
| TURN LEFT 5 steps |
| SIT for 3 seconds |
| STAND in place |
| TURN RIGHT 5 steps |
| STOP |

## Example 7: Simple app development

| Challenge name | Creating your first app |
|---|---|
| What is our challenge? | Your challenge is to design an app that will show off an area of interest or skill. It could be your favourite sport, your favourite lollies, tourism in your favourite place, or anything you are interested in. |
| How can we find out about it? | • Research your topic and collect images in a folder.<br>• Research simple app design using Jotform or similar within our microlearnings. |
| How can we design a solution? | Once research is completed, use a mind map to work out logical paths and patterns for your app. Name each page or section of your app and list what will be contained in each page. Make sure you have the most important information in the most logical locations.<br><br>Use no more than three fonts and three colours, and make sure they all work together.<br><br>What will you call your app so that it stands out? |
| What can we create? | • A mind map online or on paper<br>• A structure for the app<br>• A user guide with screen shots to show your learning and make it easier for people to use your app |
| How can we show our learning? | • Creation of the app<br>• Your original diagram with explanations |
| Microlearnings | • Mind map<br>• Simple app development |

## Example 8: Simple classification of objects

| Challenge name | Simple classification |
|---|---|
| What is our challenge? | Present a group of objects and ask students to create a classification system that would categorise these objects. The items could be:<br>• Shoes<br>• Shells<br>• Clothing items<br>• Cards with animal or plant images on them. |

| Challenge name | Simple classification |
|---|---|
| How can we find out about it? | Questions to consider:<br>• What is classification?<br>• How do we decide on which ways to classify objects?<br>• With our chosen set of objects, what would be some good classifications? |
| How can we design a solution? | 1. Brainstorm categories for your set of objects<br>2. Create a mind map for your chosen objects showing categories. |
| What can we create? | • A mind map or diagram of the structure for your classification<br>• Labelled photos and/or video showcasing your classification design and the reasons behind it |
| How can we show our learning? | • Discussion with the teacher showcasing classification or mind map<br>• Testing – if we add another item into your classification, where would it be placed and why? |

## Example 9: Cardboard automaton

| Challenge name | Cardboard automaton |
|---|---|
| What is our challenge? | Using cardboard, skewers, glue, tape and paint, create an automaton that shows motion. |
| How can we find out about it? | Science Buddies: "Make cardboard automata."<br>https://www.sciencebuddies.org/stem-activities/cardboard-automata<br>• Research automatons and how they move.<br>• Look at simple movement and examples. |
| How can we design a solution? | Design several different variations with simple moving parts and look at the way that the driving mechanism needs to work to support the movement you have decided on. |
| What can we create? | • Create the box that will house the driving mechanism (see link above).<br>• Create the driving mechanism.<br>• Add this to the box structure and check basic movement.<br>• Create the parts that will need to be added to the top of the mechanism.<br>• Paint appropriately once the design has been created. |

| How can we show our learning? | • Present design diagrams.<br>• Make finished automaton. |
|---|---|
| Microlearnings | Kinetic basics |

## Example 10: Exploring coding in Scratch

| Challenge name | Introduction to Scratch coding (Grade 1 to middle school) |
|---|---|
| What is our challenge? | To develop students' computational thinking through the development of coding skills. The important part of this is a guided focus on development of the students' skills. |
| How can we find out about it? | Developing skills through microlearnings will allow students to build knowledge in a way that forms a basis for all future learnings.<br><br>There are also many YouTube videos for further skills, but it is essential that base components are completed before continuing. |
| How can we design a solution? | 1. The skills development includes:<br>• Basic sprites<br>• Movement with arrows<br>• Collisions with sprites<br>• Collisions with colour<br><br>2. Students need to draw basic designs on paper to show the levels and designs. |
| What can we create? | Students are now able to create a maze game with multiple levels. From these further skills can be developed. |
| How can we show our learning? | Showcase and share games with the class, talking about:<br>• What went well?<br>• What did not go well?<br>• How would you expand what you have done next time?<br>• What are the next steps? |
| Microlearnings | Scratch introduction |

## Example 11: Reducing screen time

| Challenge name | Let's go outside |
|---|---|
| What is our challenge? | Parents and teachers are concerned about students having too much screen time and not going outside to explore the world around them or learning other skills that will help them in their future lives.<br><br>Your job is to create a product or system that will encourage children to be active and motivated to learn new things or be outside. |
| How can we find out about it? | Questions to consider:<br>• Who do you need to aim this at? What is their age? What are their interests?<br>• How could you look at different ways to get children away from screens and looking at other things?<br>• What can you find online that has worked?<br><br>Discuss this with your classmates to find some possible solutions. |
| How can we design a solution? | 1. Brainstorm some possible ideas.<br>2. Vote within your team and decide on one of your options.<br>3. Create a mind map or image of what that would be and how it would work. |
| What can we create? | • Work on a detailed solution and design variations (different options) that could be created. This could be different sizes, colours, designs, locations and so on.<br>• Make sure that the original target customer (person you are designing for) would like it. |
| How can we show our learning? | • Create a detailed labelled drawing or a simple prototype of your solution.<br>• Present this to a small group and get their feedback. |

## Example 12: Simple items made better

| Challenge name | Simple items made better |
|---|---|
| What is our challenge? | Your challenge is to take a simple item found around your home or your school and either add to it or change it in some way so that it works better or does something extra. |

| Challenge name | Simple items made better |
|---|---|
| How can we find out about it? | Research online and brainstorm different uses for simple items. Insider: "ButterUp knife will save your bread." https://www.youtube.com/watch?v=UNAwc_ES8m4 |
| How can we design a solution? | 1. Design and brainstorm within your group some items that could be improved or modified.<br><br>2. Think about the person that would need this item and design the item for them.<br><br>3. Reduce the number of items down to one, and research if there are similar items to this that already exist. |
| What can we create? | • Create several basic designs on paper for your product or process.<br>• Create variations that will suit the person you are designing for.<br>• Continue to refine or simplify. |
| How can we show our learning? | • Showcase your design process<br>• What did you do well?<br>• What do you still have questions about?<br>• What would you do differently next time?<br>• Create a prototype with variations and explanations to share with your class. |

## Example 13: Data gathering

| Challenge name | Data gathering |
|---|---|
| What is our challenge? | Your challenge is to look at a process within the school and see if you can gather and present data on it, then give solutions for fixing any issue. |
| How can we find out about it? | Decide on a system that is not working well or that you would like to understand better:<br>• Canteen lines<br>• Traffic flow at pick-up or drop-off time<br>• Students' favourite subjects<br>• Voting on various topics |
| How can we design a solution? | 1. Develop a survey using microlearning skills for survey design.<br>2. Brainstorm and design this on paper first. |

| Challenge name | Data gathering |
|---|---|
| **What can we create?** | A document including graphs and tables showing:<br>• Who has given data?<br>• What are the different responses to questions?<br>• What can you create that will showcase the information? |
| **How can we show our learning?** | • Depending on the age group, data can be represented in simple paper-based graphs, but for older students, basic Excel graphing skills, as outlined in the microlearnings, are beneficial.<br>• Students can then create a PowerPoint to present their learnings to their teacher or the class. |
| **Microlearnings** | • Survey creation<br>• Data analysis (Excel) |

# PART 5
# MICROLEARNINGS AND SKILL DEVELOPMENT

"Let us pick up our books and our pens. They are our most powerful weapons. One child, one teacher, one book and one pen can change the world."

– MALALA YOUSAFZAI

In this part, basic skills helpful for STEAM authenticity are shown. This can be considered as information to support your students or as professional learning for educators. The idea is to make it as straightforward and as logical as possible, while helping to build the required skills. These chapters are meant to be dipped into as needed, rather than read as a whole.

The term "microlearning" relates to creating short, sharp, logical chunks of learning that are given at the right time and in the right way to achieve success. Within this book, and on the website, the microlearnings are placed into the following categories:

- Algorithm and structure
- Coding
- Virtual and augmented reality
- General skills.

In the same way that your students need to learn these concepts, so do you. Use them as needed, when needed, and in the way that you need them. This is the best way to complete skill-building. Over time it becomes second nature, and while at the time the development of small pockets of information may seem insignificant, over time there will be an in-depth transfer of knowledge.

CHAPTER 16

# Algorithms, mind maps and structure

## Algorithms

Understanding algorithms is essential to 21st-century learning. They involve creating a series of steps in a particular order that help you to make decisions. It is a great idea, even for younger students, to use the word algorithm rather than simplifying. Some examples of where algorithms occur in our lives are:

- Making a cake
- Going to the supermarket and buying everything on your list
- Making a paper airplane
- Catching the bus to school.

Here are some great conversation starters:

- "Algorithms are part of our world. You deal with them in every part of your life every day; you just do not necessarily realise it." Show an example of this YouTube clip from "The Big Bang Theory": https://www.youtube.com/watch?v=k0xgjUhEG3U.
- "Think of this morning. When you woke up, you decided whether it was a school day or not. If it is a school day, you get up; if not, you stay in bed." This simple algorithm could be represented like this:

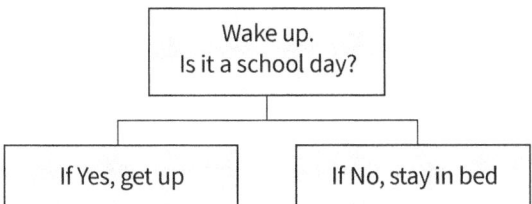

An example of a task that could be presented to the students:

## PowerPoint hot spots

In pairs, create an algorithm for a "choose your own adventure" story. This can be done on paper or using Inspiration or PowerPoint. One of the paths needs to be at least five choices long. The algorithm might start to look like this:

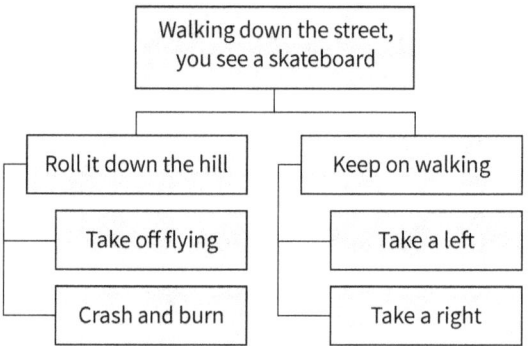

Sample of how this might look:  Leads to:
 I select "Roll down the hill":

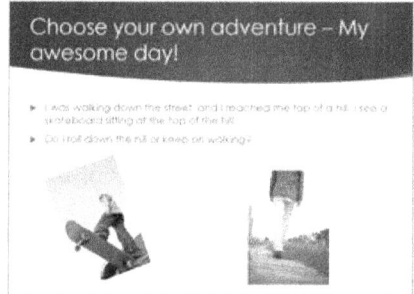 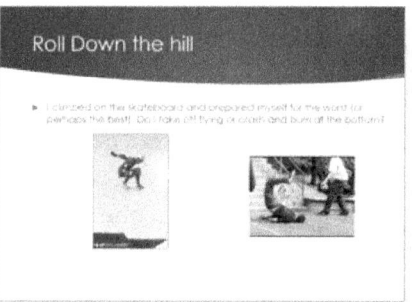

Continue as required for each choice on the screen. Students will need to be methodical and cross off pages as they are completed and linked, as it can get confusing.

## Algorithm design using data flow diagrams

It is possible to draw diagrams of algorithms using the symbols on the next page. These diagrams are called data flow diagrams:

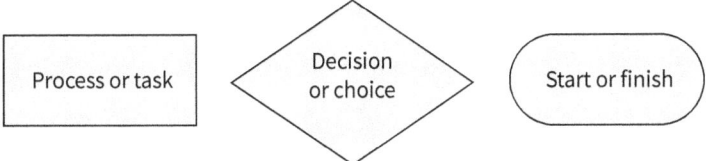

Here is a simple example of a data flow diagram:

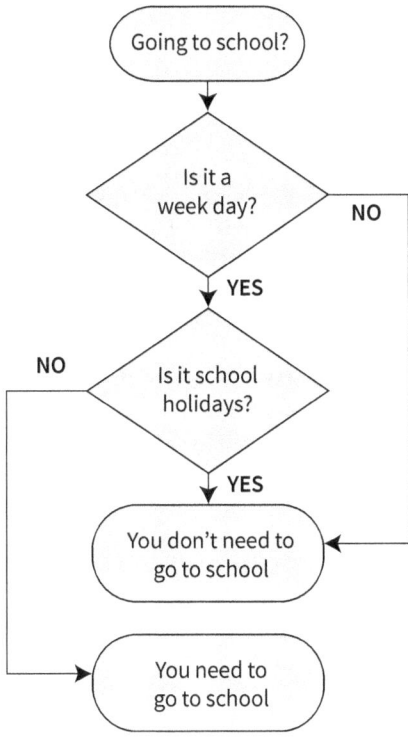

You are encouraged to be as creative as possible – your story does not need to be realistic!

## Hyperlinking in PowerPoint

Using clip art or photos

1. Insert the clip art you wish to link to.

2. Click on it with your right mouse button. The following screen will appear:

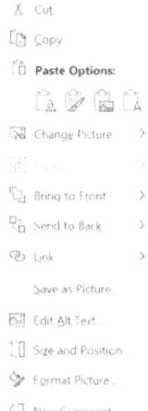

3. Select **Link**. The following screen will appear:

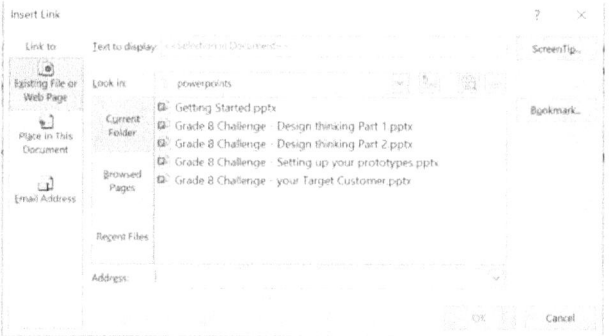

4. Click on **Place in This Document**. The following screen will appear:

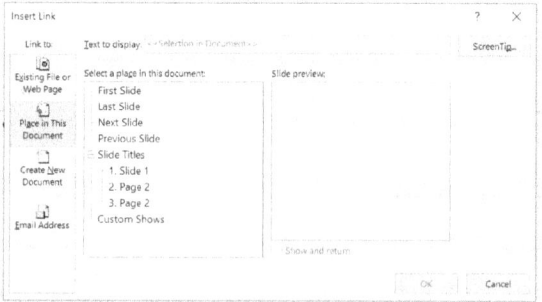

5. Select the page you want to link to.

6. Click on OK.

## Adding a button

1. From the Insert menu, select **SmartArt**. The following screen will appear:

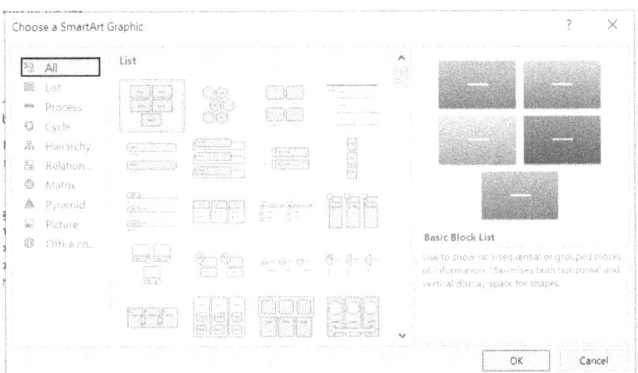

2. Click on the **Basic Block List** button. The following should appear:

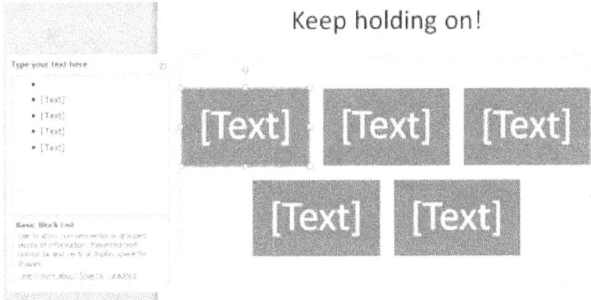

3. Click into the box on the left-hand side and delete all but one of the dot points.
4. Type in the text you want to be in the box.
5. Resize the box, then click out of it.
6. Repeat as necessary.

## Adding a hyperlinked picture

1. In the **Insert** menu, click on either **Smart Art** or **Pictures**.
2. Select a picture and place it in the PowerPoint document.
3. Resize the picture if necessary.

4. Right-click on the picture. The following menu will appear:

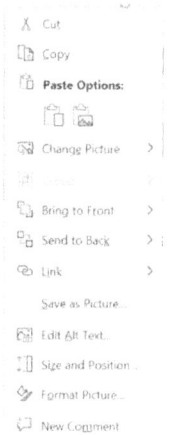

5. Select **Link**. The following dialog will appear:

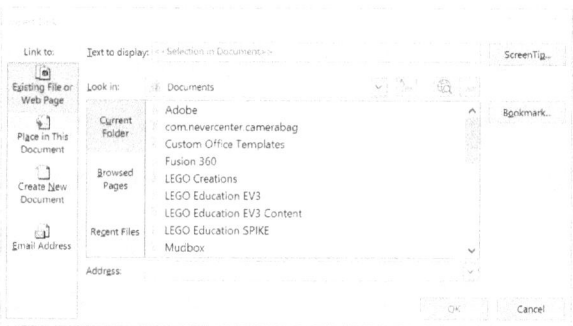

6. Click on **Place in This Document**, select the page, and click on OK.

# Mind maps

## *Getting started*

A mind map is a visual way to represent brainstorming or help to understand the relationships between concepts, events or ideas. We can use mind maps to:

- Clarify thinking
- Develop ideas and pathways
- Show understanding.

The process of visualisation and the physical creation of the content allows students to develop a clear understanding of the concept.

Mind maps can be created using:

- Word (SmartArt)
- Paper
- Inspiration
- Mind Mup (https://www.mindmup.com).

The sample shown here is from Mind Mup, but many different options are available. Whichever you use, the clear need is to put concepts into ordered categories. This will help to break down information into manageable categories.

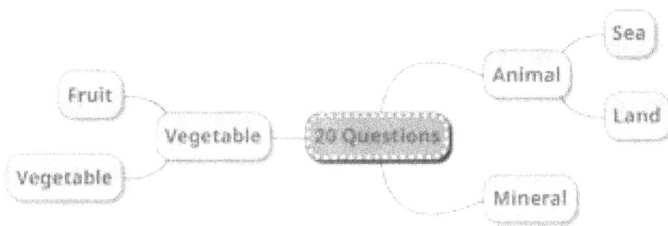

CHAPTER 17

# Coding

Coding is a key concept that is essential for 21st-century learners, but is also one in which many educators have minimal background. At its core, coding is about problem-solving and breaking down problems into manageable pieces.

There are many ways that coding can be used within STEAM education. Each has its own value and place. However, the overall approach is what is important. It is essential that key concepts are covered in a specific way to develop students' computational thinking.

Within this chapter, the focus is on:

- Scratch
- Microbits.

## Scratch introduction

One of the most important elements when teaching coding is to have a clear idea of the skills people need to understand programming and to be able to develop skills further on their own. This is just a basic introduction with some future pathways and resources to help develop from that point onwards.

Some conversation starters:

- A lot of modern programs are set up to be "object oriented". This basically means that if you click on something, something will happen. If you do not click on the button, that code will never be executed. This is a term you will see a lot if you are going to begin programming, and it applies to a lot of websites, languages and apps.
- For example, in Word, if you highlight some text, then click on the bold button, it will change the highlighted area to **Bold**. This is an example

of object-oriented programming that you see all the time but take for granted.

## Getting started
- You can use Scratch online from http://scratch.mit.edu
- You will need to create a login account. Once this is created, click on the **Create** button.

After you have completed each task, check to make sure it works, then move on. A great way to start programming in Scratch is by creating a maze game. By doing each step in order, you will be able to build up skills, from simple to hard.

Note: The **Tutorials** tab is very useful to build skills and gain understanding that can be used in later challenges.

## Inserting and resizing
1. A sprite is an image that will be your player or component within the space. There could be one or many. The option to add sprites is at the bottom right-hand corner of the screen:

2. To add a sprite, click on the **Choose a Sprite** button. The following screen will appear:

3. Select your chosen sprite from the options available. This will insert your sprite into the program.
4. If you wish to delete a sprite, select the sprite, then click on the rubbish bin at the top right-hand corner of the screen.
5. When working with sprites, it is important to understand that the sprite you have selected is the sprite that has code added to it. That code will only work with that sprite. To code another sprite, click on the correct sprite and begin work.
6. To create a background, click on the **Choose a Background** button. The following screen will appear:

7. Select one of the backgrounds shown, or upload your own image.

## *Understanding menu options*

Scratch will follow the commands given to it. At the left-hand side of the screen is a vertical menu strip containing all of the menu options:

Following is a table describing some of the key components under the different menu options to get started.

| Menu | Component | Description |
|---|---|---|
| Motion | move 10 steps | Will move the sprite the desired number of steps. Will move the sprite in the direction it is facing. |
| | turn ↻ 15 degrees<br>turn ↺ 15 degrees | Will turn the sprite the desired number of degrees, either clockwise or anticlockwise. |
| | change x by 10<br>change y by 10 | Uses x (horizontal) and y (vertical) to adjust position. |
| Looks | say Hello! for 2 seconds<br>say Hello!<br>think Hmm for 2 seconds<br>think Hmm | These blocks will show either a thought or a speech bubble. Text and timeframes can be changed. |
| | switch costume to costume2 ▾<br>next costume | Costumes can refer to literal clothing or to movement. Available costumes for each sprite can be accessed by selecting the **Costumes** tab at the top left-hand corner of the screen. It will appear as below:<br><br>It is also possible to use the tools shown on this page to modify or add to "costumes". |
| | switch backdrop to backdrop1 ▾<br>next backdrop | Allows the change to a different backdrop. This might be useful for changes in levels, or visits to different rooms. |

| Menu | Component | Description |
| --- | --- | --- |
| | change size by 10 / set size to 100 % | This size change is useful within games. For example, if food is "eaten", the sprite might grow. If energy is expelled, the sprite might shrink. |
| Events | | The code below these sections will only be activated if the green flag, or appropriate keyboard button (e.g. space bar), is selected. |
| | | These are "on click" events activated by clicking on the sprite or looking at a change in the backdrop. The code will only be activated if the events occur. |
| Control | wait 1 seconds | Will create a wait option. |
| | repeat 10 | Will repeat the content of the component a required number of times. |
| | forever | Will repeat the content forever. |
| | if then | Used when a choice is required. For example, if the ball hits the sprite, what will happen? |
| Sensing | touching / color is touching color | These two relate directly to maze options and can be used, for example, when a sprite touches the edge of the maze. |
| | ask What's your name? and wait | This can be used to ask for and store responses. The question can be changed. |
| | key space ▼ pressed? | Can be used when various buttons are pressed. |

134   Creating Authenticity in STEAM Education

## Moving sprites

1. To get sprites to move, we need to select the code below and drop it onto the workspace. All code snippets are colour-coded for the menu they are found in.

2. To move sprites with arrows, use the code below:

3. Some key points:
   - X direction creates horizontal movement, and Y direction creates vertical movement.
   - Putting a negative number in the white box will produce movement downwards or to the left.

## Collisions with sprites

1. Select two sprites (e.g. cat and mouse).
2. Select the cat, then complete the code below:

3. The bottom code will move the cat back by 15 and say "Meow" as it does so. Because of the forever loop, this will happen time and again until the game finishes.

## Collisions with colour

If creating a maze, it is possible to set up a coloured maze, as well as obstacles. Collisions with colour can be very useful. Here is how to use them:

## To run your code

To run the code, click on the green **Go** flag at the top of the screen.

## Where to from here?

To continue from here and make your maze, focus on the following skills:

- Create a background with a drawn maze in a set colour. Draw on paper first if needed. One easy option is to create a square (or other shape in a set colour) and then use the eraser to build a path through the colour block.
- Make sure the sprite is sized to fit comfortably within the path you create, or you will have constant collisions with the edge of the maze.
- At the end of the first background, place a colour or sprite, and set up a collision so that the collision triggers access to the next background.

- Reset the position on the second background to be at the start of the next maze.
- Have lots of fun!

## Microbit introduction

The Microbit is a tiny programmable device (about half the size of a credit card) that allows students to get hands-on with coding and digital making.

### Getting started with the Microbit

1. Visit https://makecode.microbit.org/. The following screen will appear:

2. Click on the **New Project** button. The following screen will appear:

3. Type in an appropriate name for the project, then click on **Create**. The following screen will appear:

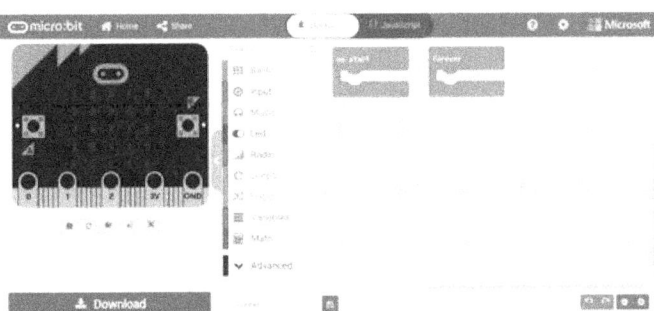

4. From the **Basic** menu, drag the elements across to make the code look as shown below:

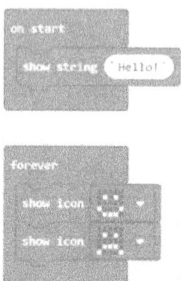

5. Now modify the code to change the timing and output:

6. To run on the simulator, click on the ▶ at the left-hand side of the screen. Alternatively, download to the Microbit. To do this, complete the following tasks:
   i. Connect the Microbit to a USB port on your computer via a cable.
   ii. Depending on which version of the Microbit you have, either click on **Pair** or see below:
   iii. Click on the **Download** button.
   iv. The following image will appear at the bottom left-hand corner of the screen.

   v. Use the file explorer to drag and drop the file onto the Microbit, which will appear as though it were a USB. It will now work on the Microbit.

7. Keep modifying the code to change the following options to whatever you would like:

| Element | How to use it |
|---|---|
| show leds | Click on each of the boxes to make your pattern. If you put it within code (e.g. on start) it will show your pattern on the simulator. |
| on shake | If you put code inside **on shake** it will change to that code whenever you shake the Microbit. Click on the drop-down arrow to the right of **shake** and explore the other available options. shake, logo up, logo down, screen up, screen down, tilt left, tilt right, free fall, 3g, 6g, 8g |
| on button A pressed (A, B, A+B) | Add code within this element to get different options to occur depending on what is pressed. When button A is pressed, one set of code will be activated. When button B is pressed, another set of code will be activated. When A+B (i.e. both buttons at the same time) are pressed, another set of code will be activated. |
| repeat 4 times do | This code will repeat whatever is within it the number of times you indicate (in this case four times). |

Coding   139

## Practising events

Create a program that will put up different images depending on what you do with it. For example, shake, click button A, click button B, and so on.

## Create a dice

We need three pieces of code: one to detect a throw (shake), another to pick a random number, and then one to show the number.

1. Place the **on shake** block onto the editor workspace. It runs code when you shake the Microbit.

2. Create the following code. This will show a number when the Microbit is shaken.

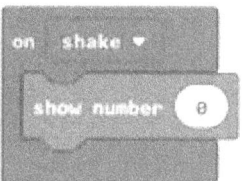

3. To set up a random number, select a **pick random** block as below:

4. Change the numbers in the **pick random** box to 1 and 6 respectively.

5. Use the simulator to try out your code. Does it show the number you expected?

6. If you have a Microbit connected, click **Download** and transfer your code to the Microbit. Use the diagram below to help you.

## True or false – using the IF statement

1. Get the following block from the **Input** section.

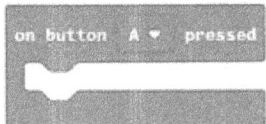

2. Grab an **if else** block and set it inside the block. Put a **pick random true or false** into the **if** as its condition. As shown below:

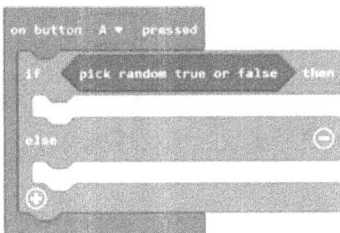

3. Now put a **show icon** block inside both the **if** and the **else**. Pick images to mean true and false (this could also be heads and tails).

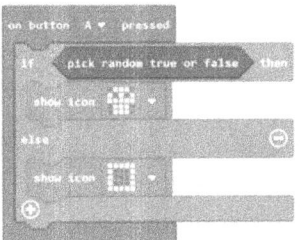

# Microbit input detection

Microbits are worth exploring for their many and varied challenges. They can detect:

- Speed
- Temperature
- Light detection
- Sound detection
- Compass direction.

These can be used in a variety of ways and open themselves up to some excellent open-ended STEAM challenges. An example where it could be used effectively is with smart clothing. Smart clothing is clothing that interacts with the wearer to give various readings.

To create smart clothing options, an e-textiles set (Kitronik 5607) can be added:
https://kitronik.co.uk/products/5607-e-textiles-kit-for-the-bbc-microbit.

## *Heat, light and sound*

Coding for heat, light and sound is simple, as the Microbit can detect temperature easily. This links quite well into the science course for Grade 9 science.

Basic coding details for each of these components are shown below:

| Coding | Used to detect |
|---|---|
| on button B ▼ pressed / show number temperature (°C) | Detects temperature in degrees Celsius but can be converted to degrees Fahrenheit or Kelvin. This could be used to create a thermometer, or used on clothing to indicate the sportsperson is getting too warm. |
| on button A ▼ pressed / show number light level | Checks for light level. This can be adjusted to make night lights or sun sensors to place on hats or clothing. |
| on button A+B ▼ pressed / show number sound level | Will measure sound levels and show on Microbits. Could be used to detect sound levels in decibels. |

## Movement

| Coding | Used to |
|---|---|
| 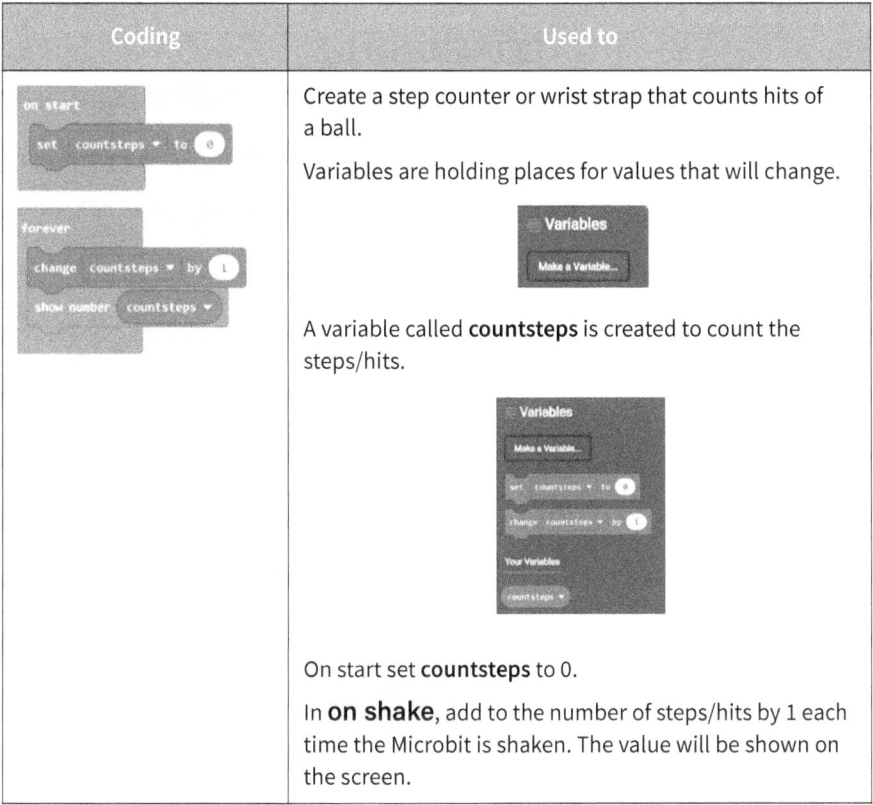 | Create a step counter or wrist strap that counts hits of a ball. Variables are holding places for values that will change. A variable called **countsteps** is created to count the steps/hits. On start set **countsteps** to 0. In **on shake**, add to the number of steps/hits by 1 each time the Microbit is shaken. The value will be shown on the screen. |

CHAPTER 18

# Virtual and augmented reality

## Meta Spark

### Installing and opening

1. Click on or type in the following link: https://sparkar.facebook.com/ar-studio/. The following screen will appear:

2. Click on the **Get Started** button.
3. Once logged in, you will see:

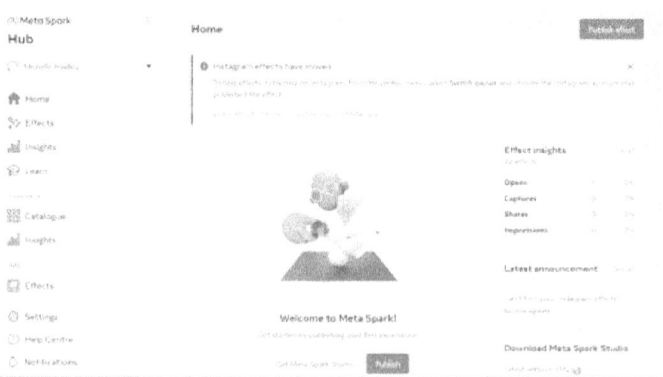

4. The following dialog will appear:

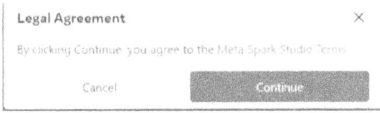

5. Click on **Continue**.

## Starting Meta Spark

1. Click on **Start**, then **Meta Spark Studio v162**. The following screen will appear:

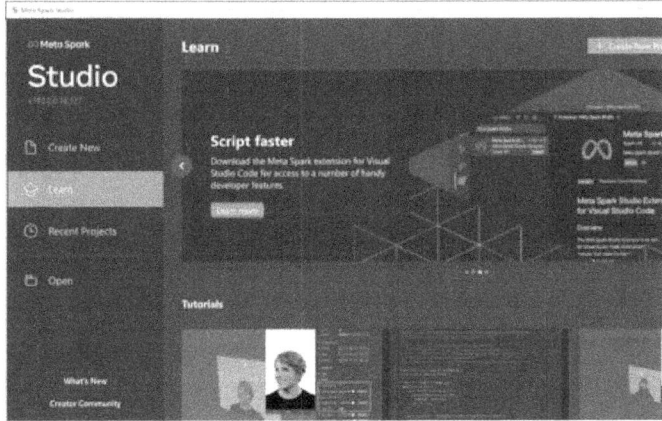

2. Click on the **+ Create New Project** button or click on **+**. The following screen will appear:

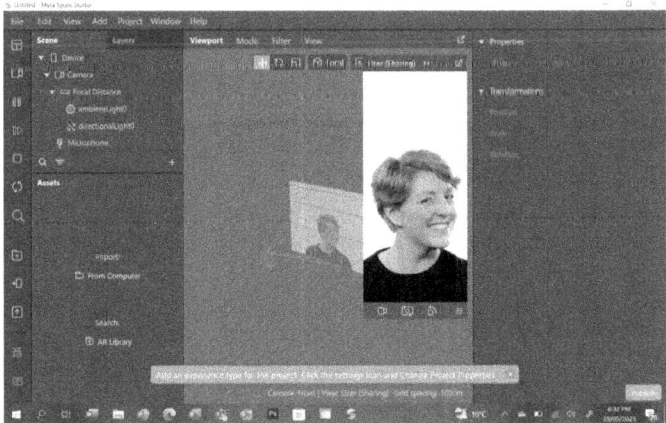

Virtual and augmented reality    145

3. To change the person, click on the camera button at the left-hand side of the screen:

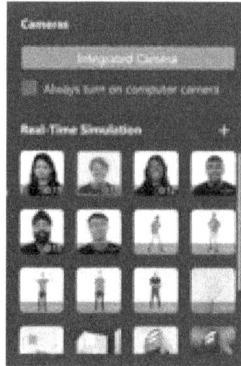

4. Click on an image to change to that image. To change to your own image, click on the tick box below. This will show your own face, and you will be able to test how effects work on you.

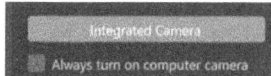

## Adding a face mesh filter

1. Click on the + sign. The following screen will appear:

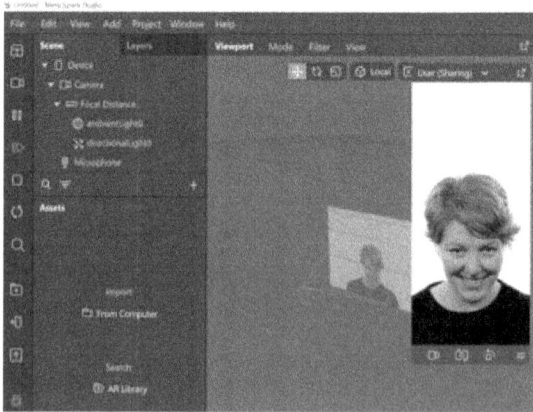

2. Make sure that you have downloaded the face reference assets using the link below:
"Face reference assets for Meta Spark Studio."
https://sparkar.facebook.com/ar-studio/learn/articles/people-tracking/face-reference-assets/

3. Click on the **+** button. The following screen will appear:

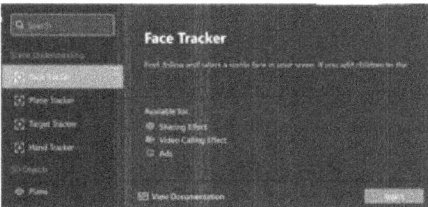

4. Scroll down to find **Face Mesh**. Click on it, then click on the **Insert** button. The following screen will appear:

5. To add our tattoos (or other images) we will need to add materials. To do so, click on the **+** to the right of the **Materials** option in the right-hand side panel. The following screen will appear:

6. A new asset will appear in the left-hand panel as below:

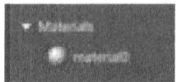

7. Rename that to Tattoo by clicking on the asset with your right-mouse button and selecting **Rename**. It will now look like:

8. Download the face reference assets from the internet and place them in a place you can find them again (e.g. on your desktop).
9. Select the face texture you wish to use – e.g.

- faceFeminine.jpg
- faceMasculine.jpg
- faceMesh.png
- faceMeshMask.png
- faceMeshTrackers.png

10. Photoshop is used to add texture in the instructions below. However, it is possible to use other simpler software apps to complete the same tasks.
11. Open the texture of your choice in a document. The following screen will appear:

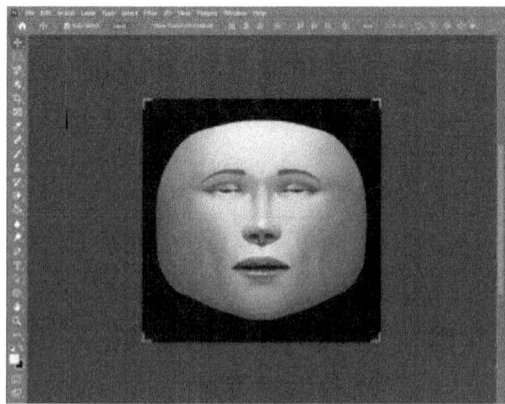

12. Insert the tattoo (or image of your choice) as a new Layer. The following screen will appear:

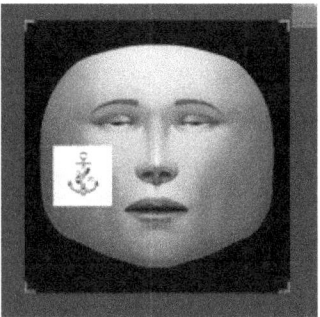

13. To map it to the face, from the **Edit** menu, choose **Transform**, then **Warp**. A grid as shown below will appear on the image:

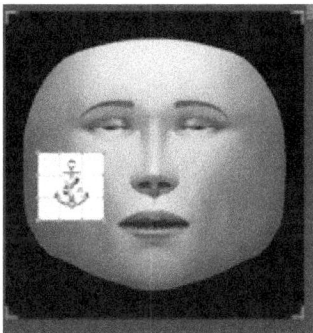

14. By grabbing the squares on the edges of the image, it is possible to map the image to the face in the layer below. It will look as below once manipulated.

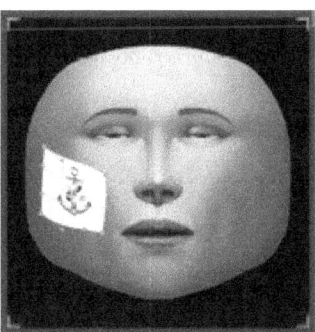

15. Turn off the back layer by clicking on the eye icon to the left of **Background** so that the face is not shown. The screen will look as below:

16. From the **File** menu, select **Export**, then **Quick Export as PNG**. The following screen will appear:

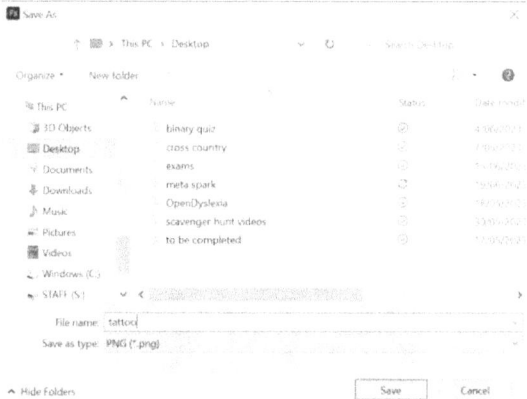

17. Save in an appropriate folder for easy retrieval.
18. Return to Meta Spark. Open the screen as below so you can see your file and the image you are trying to overlay as below:

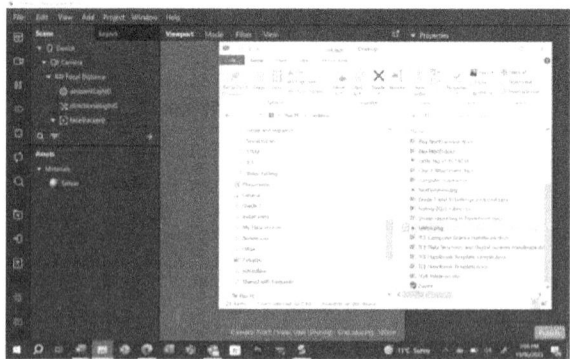

19. Drag and drop the tattoo overlay document over into the **Assets** section on the left-hand side of the screen. It will now appear as below:

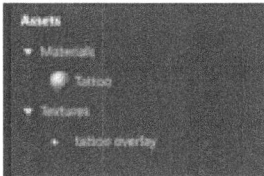

20. Click on **Tattoo** on the left-hand side. The right-hand side panel will appear as below:

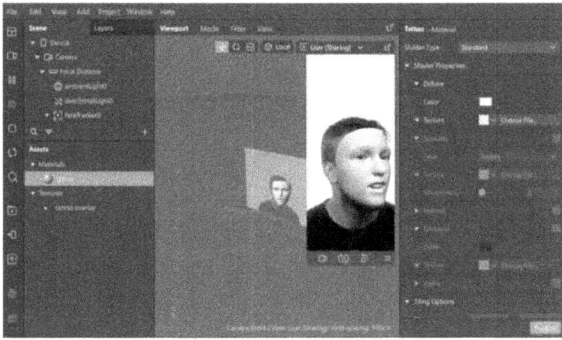

21. Click on the drop-down to the right of the **Texture** component. The following screen will appear:

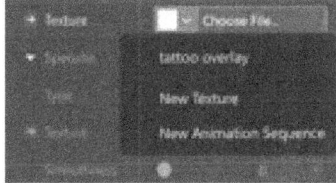

22. Select **tattoo overlay**. The image should now appear on your screen.

## Chatbots with WotNot

There are many options for creating chatbots – some programmable and some not. Many are free to start but will require payment further on. WotNot is a simple-to-use software package that does not require a credit card, has an unlimited trial, and is able to deal with quite complex branching while remaining simple to understand. It is great as an initial approach to chatbots.

Virtual and augmented reality   151

A summary of key concepts is provided below to help you get started.

## Creating a login

1. Visit https://wotnot.io. The following screen will appear:

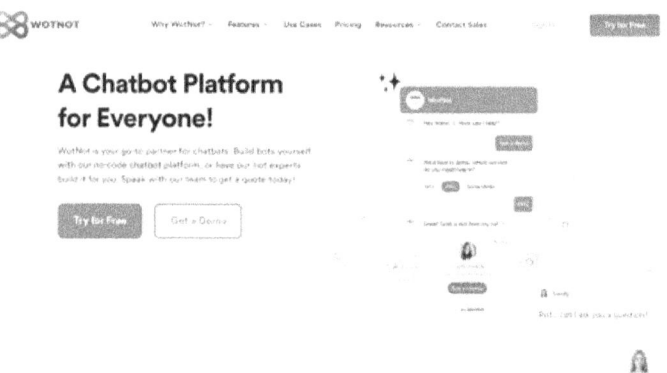

2. Click on **Try for Free** and create a login.

## Creating your first chatbot

1. When logged in, your screen will appear as below:

2. Click on the **Bot Builder** button. The following screen will appear:

3. Click on the **Build a Bot** button. The following screen will appear:

4. Select the **Build an Inbound Bot** button. The following screen will appear:

5. Select an option. This can be changed to other options later. The following screen will appear:

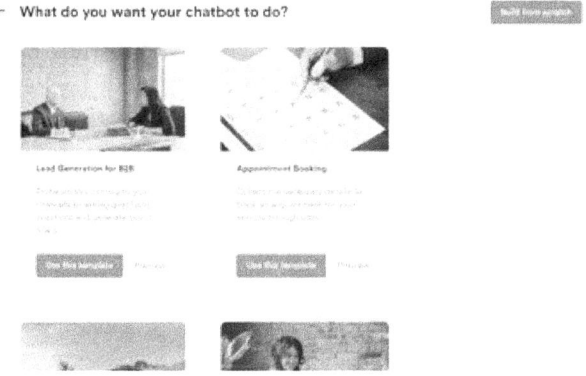

6. Click on the **Build from scratch** button. The following screen will appear:

Virtual and augmented reality    153

## Before starting

**Intention matching**

To start, it is important to think about what you want to achieve with the bot and how you are going to get that to work. You may have more than one intention for your chatbot.

Examples of intentions might be hours of operation, available products, or prices of items.

**Paper planning**

Key tasks:

1. What are the key questions a human would use to solve the problem you are trying to solve? For example, where will I go for a holiday this year?
2. Draw a data-flow diagram on paper that will allow you to reach a resolution using the questions broken down in the previous question.

   Once you have done that, you are ready to start working in WotNot (or the chatbot builder of your choice).

## Useful components

1. Rename the chatbot by clicking on the **Untitled Bot** option and typing in a new name.
2. To create the first action, click on the **+** below the current text box. The following screen will appear:

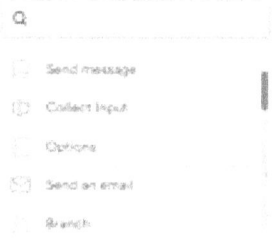

| Component | Description |
|---|---|
| Send message | This might be a message of introduction and getting started. For example:<br><br><br><br>Click on the message and to the right will appear the following screen:<br><br>Add a new title and place content. Text can be added or a file uploaded. |
| Options | Click on the **Options** button, and the following screen will appear:<br><br>If you click on this component, a section will appear at the right-hand side of the screen: |

Virtual and augmented reality   155

| Component | Description |
|---|---|
| | Fill in the heading and text as required. Then enter the options you wish to supply to your clients. 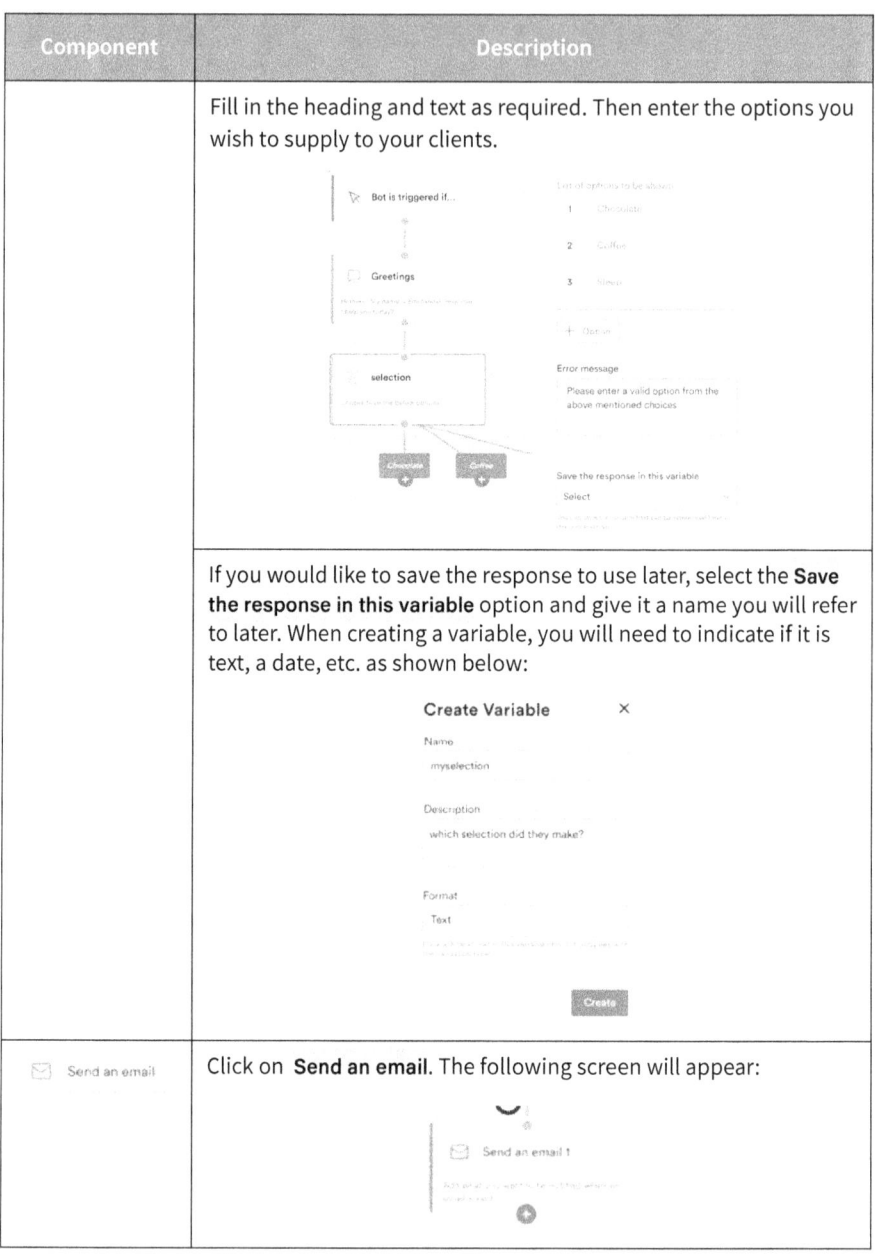 |
| | If you would like to save the response to use later, select the **Save the response in this variable** option and give it a name you will refer to later. When creating a variable, you will need to indicate if it is text, a date, etc. as shown below: |
| Send an email | Click on **Send an email**. The following screen will appear: |

156   Creating Authenticity in STEAM Education

| Component | Description |
|---|---|
| | Click on this box. The following screen will appear: <br><br>Send an email 1<br><br>Send an email to<br>name@example.com<br>CC name@example.com<br>BCC name@example.com<br>Subject<br>Lead generated via WotNot<br><br>Fill in the email, CC (carbon copy) and Subject boxes as needed. |
|  Collect Input | Click on **Collect Input**. The following screen will appear: <br><br>Collect Input 1<br><br>Click on this box. The following screen will appear: <br><br>Collect Input 1<br><br>Shows this question<br>B I U<br>What is your<br><br>Save the response in this variable<br><br>Type in the question you would like a response to. Save the response in the variable so that it can be returned to. |

| Component | Description |
|---|---|
| 📅 Calendar | Click on the **Calendar** option. The following screen will appear: 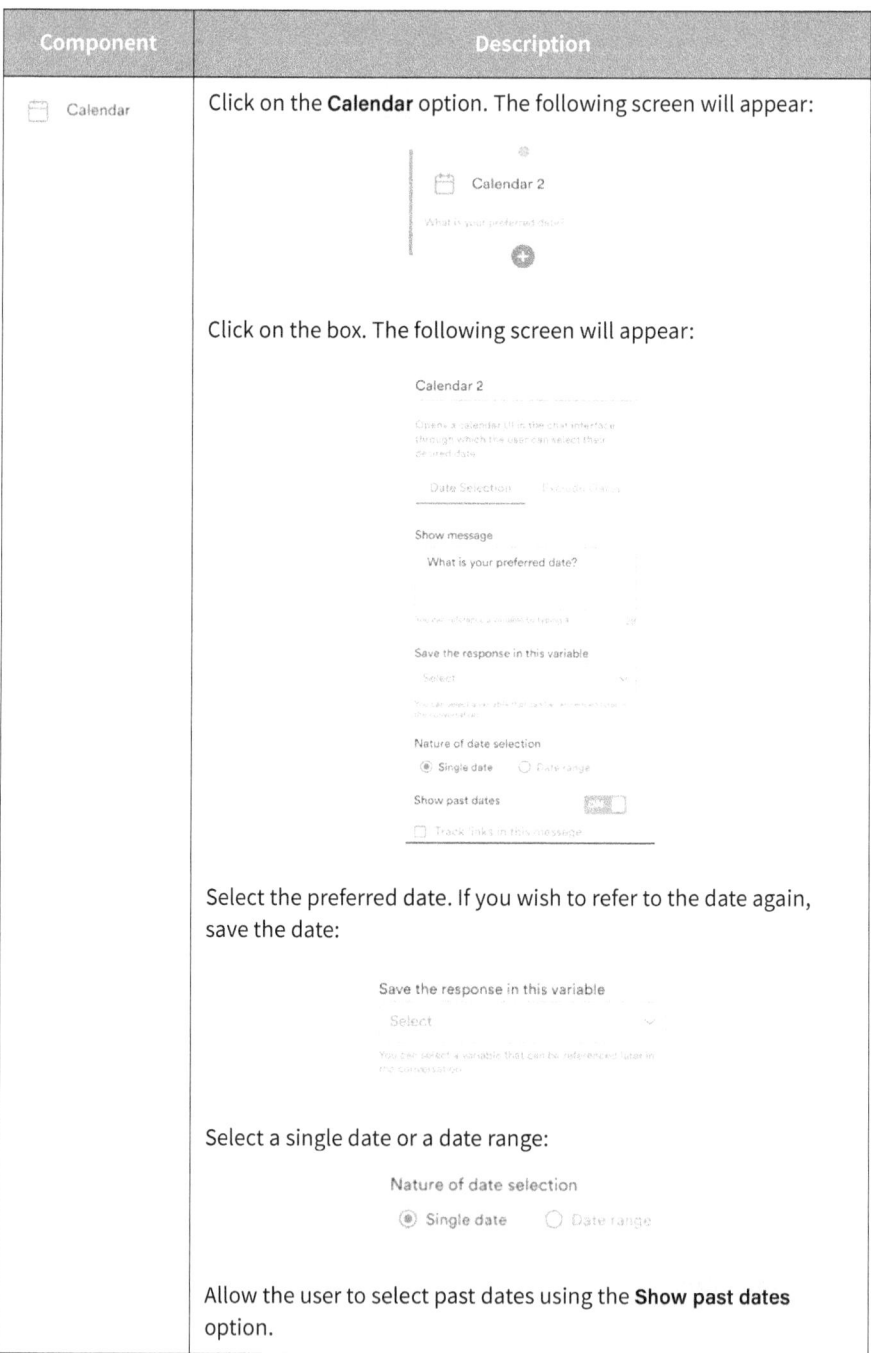 Click on the box. The following screen will appear: Select the preferred date. If you wish to refer to the date again, save the date: Select a single date or a date range: Allow the user to select past dates using the **Show past dates** option. |

| Component | Description |
|---|---|
| Buttons | Click on the **Buttons** option. The following screen will appear: 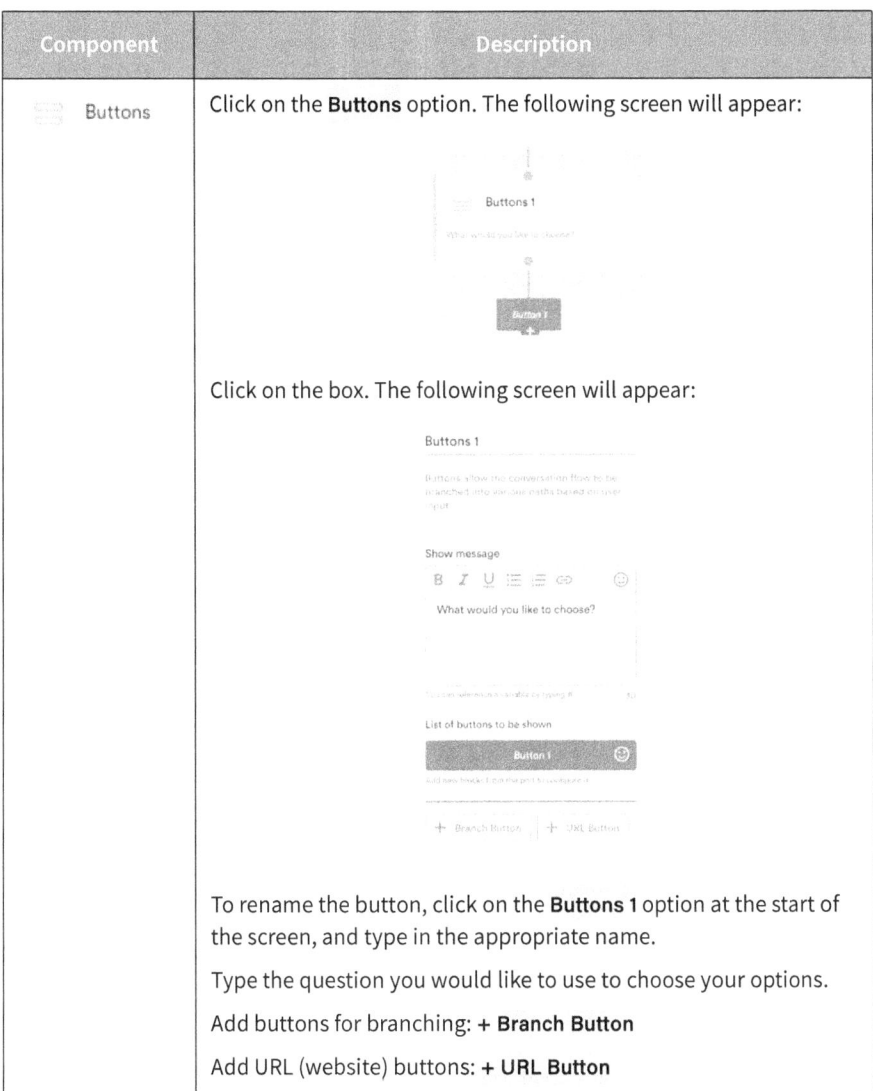 Click on the box. The following screen will appear: To rename the button, click on the **Buttons 1** option at the start of the screen, and type in the appropriate name. Type the question you would like to use to choose your options. Add buttons for branching: **+ Branch Button** Add URL (website) buttons: **+ URL Button** |

Virtual and augmented reality 159

## Testing the chatbot

Your chatbot can be tested at any time. To test your bot:

1. Click on **Test this bot**. The following screen will appear:

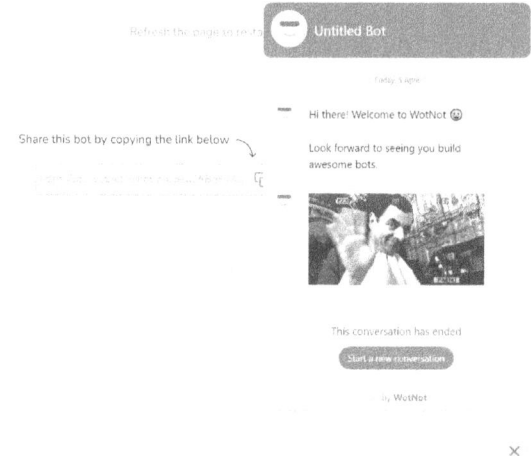

2. To start testing the chatbot, click on the smiley face. The first item from the chatbot will appear. Follow the steps of the bot to completion.
3. Change if necessary and then repeat the testing process.
4. To use the chatbot externally, click on the copy button:

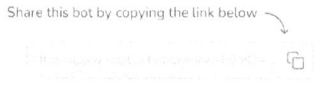

This can then be used anywhere that can access the link.

# General and presentation skills

# Video editing

## Getting started

There are a huge number of apps and programs available for video creation. The following content focuses on the simple video options available on PCs.

Simple videos are a great way to give a quick snapshot of solutions to tasks. To create them well, however, there are some simple guidelines that should always be followed. These are:

- Keep videos less than 3 minutes long when possible.
- Have a simple and clear title page.
- Plan audio and video when possible, using a comic strip or dot point planning style.
- Sound quality is important. This may mean recording sound separately with a decent microphone and/or recording within a space with minimal background noise or echo.

## *Screen recording*

Screen recording can be used to give instructions or show details of digital solutions. This can be a very useful tool and can be completed very efficiently. It is a great way to showcase a product or explain a concept. One of the easiest ways to do this is using PowerPoint:

1. Open the content you wish to record.
2. Open PowerPoint, go to **New**, and click on the **Blank Presentation** button.
3. The following screen will appear:

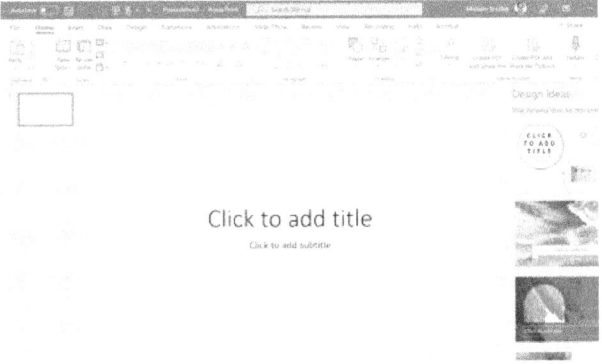

4. Click on the **Record** tab. The following screen will appear:

5. To record the screen, click on **Screen Recording**. The following toolbar will appear at the top of the screen:

6. Click on the **Select Area** button, then click and drag the area of the screen you wish to record.
7. When ready to record, click on **Record**. The screen will show 3, 2, 1 and then the recording will start.
8. Record the audio and move through the document as needed for recording.
9. To pause the video, click on **Pause**.
10. To restart the video, click on **Record**.
11. To stop the video, click on the **Stop** button.
12. Return to PowerPoint. The screen recording will be there as below:

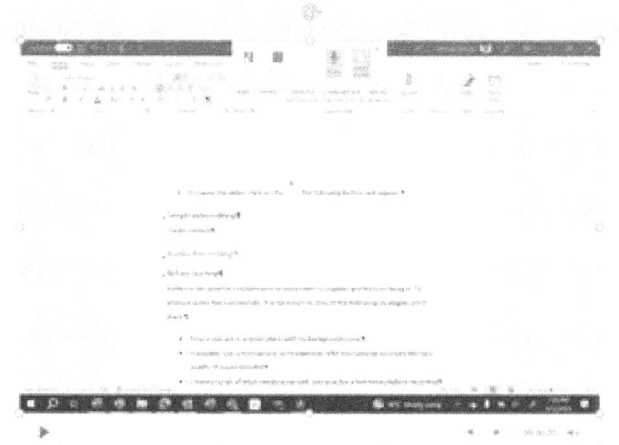

13. To play and test the recording, click on the ▶ button at the bottom of the screen.
14. To save the file as an MP4, right-click on the recording. The following screen will appear:

15. Select the **Save Media as...** button. The **Save as** screen will appear. Save as required.

## Simple video editing

The method for recording is not important – students may use phones (if school restrictions allow this) or computers, and can use any format they choose. The instructions below are for the new PC program Clipchamp.

1. Click on **Microsoft Clipchamp** to begin. The following screen will appear:

2. Click on the **Create a new video** option to start. The following screen will appear:

Virtual and augmented reality   163

3. To add content such as images or videos, click on **Import media**. The following screen will appear:

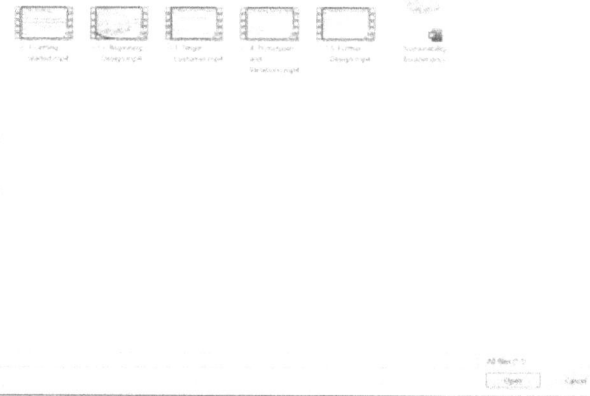

4. Import as required, then click on **Open**. Repeat as necessary. The following screen will appear:

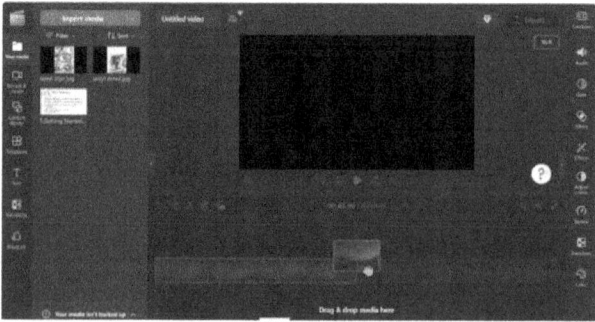

5. To add items to the timeline, either drag and drop the item to the timeline or click on the **+** to the right of the images. The screen will appear as below:

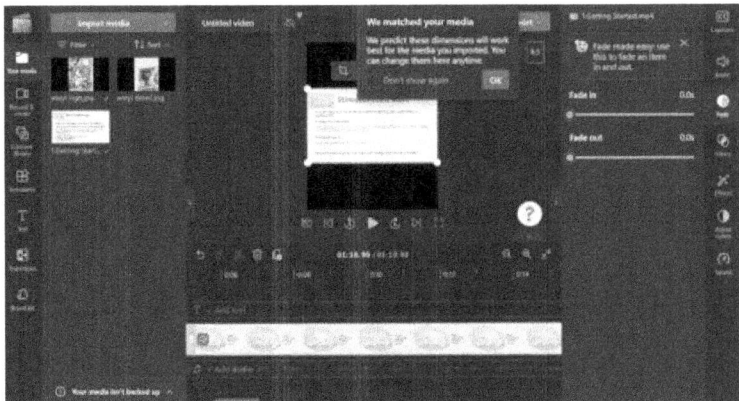

6. Some of the available options are:

| Button | Functionality |
|---|---|
| | Adds automatic captioning to the imported file. |
| | Allows audio to be increased, decreased, or detached from video. |
| | Allows fade in and fade out to be added to the video for an adjustable number of seconds. |

Virtual and augmented reality 165

| Button | Functionality |
|---|---|
| | Offers several variations of filters to be added to the video. |
| | Offers several variations of effects to be added to the video. |
| | Offers colour adjustment and reset of colour. |
| | Allows adjustment of speed of the video. |

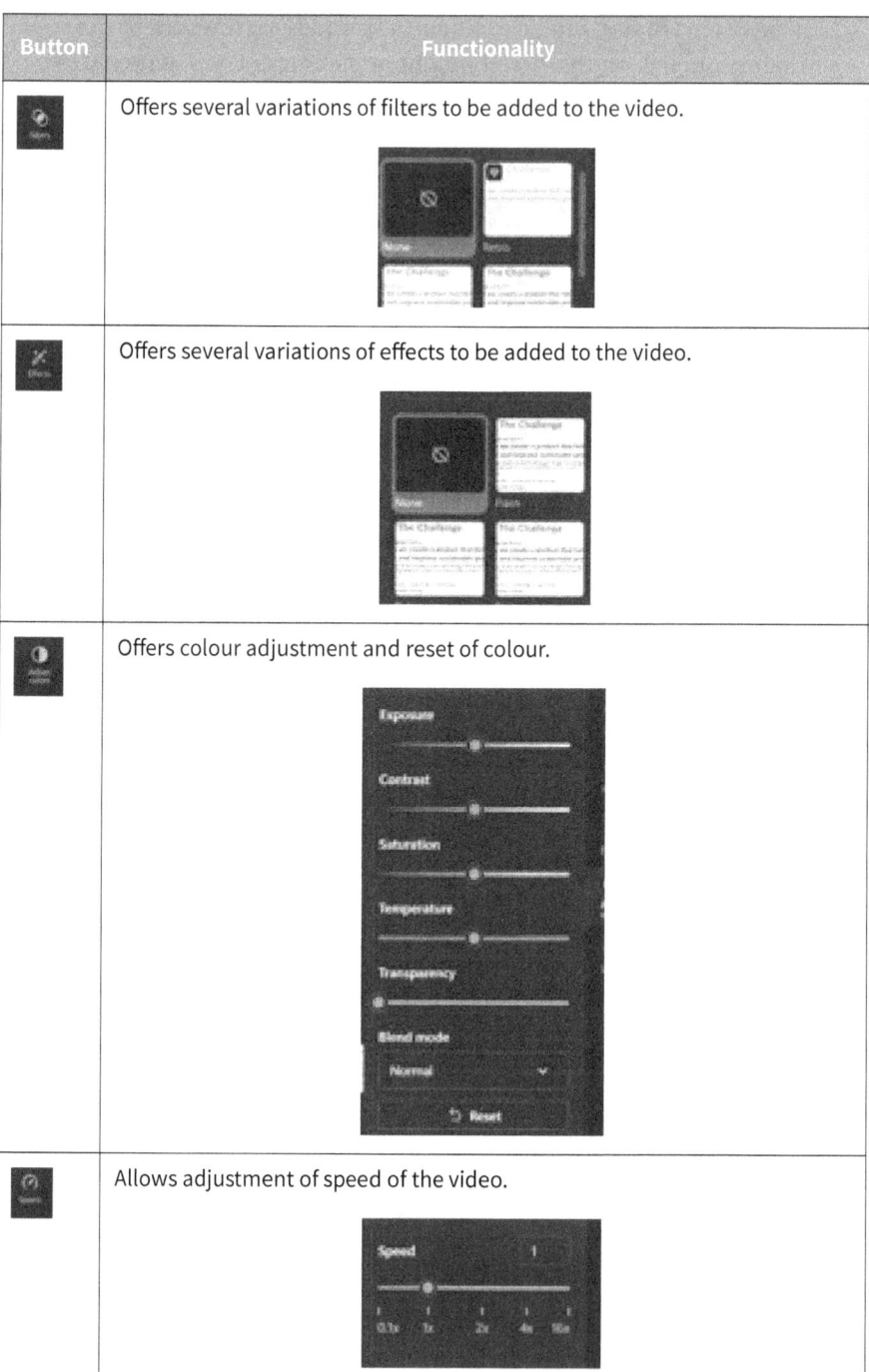

7. To add audio, import the media file, then drag and drop it to the **Add audio** section of the timeline.
8. To complete video, click on the **Export** button. The following screen will appear:

9. Click on the appropriate option, then the following screen will appear:

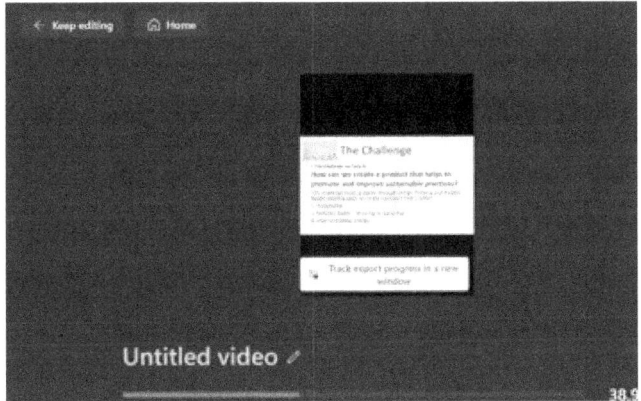

10. Type in a new name for the video. When completed, the following screen will appear:

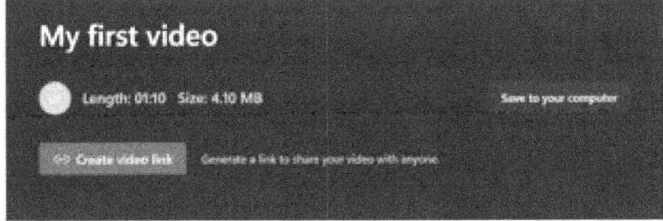

11. It is possible to save the file to your computer or add a video link from this screen.

# Audio recording

## Before starting

Audio can be used for catchphrases or voice-overs to support products or designs. To produce audio files successfully, it is necessary to ensure the following strategies are in place:

- Ensure you are in a quiet place with no background noise.
- If possible, use a microphone or headphones with a built-in microphone to create the best sound quality possible.
- Create a script of what needs to be said, and practise a few times before recording.
- Keep the content and length as concise as possible to ensure listeners' interest is maintained.
- Avoid the use of jargon and match the content to your audience's ability and experience.

## Creating audio

The Voice Recorder app is available on most PCs.

1. Ensure you are in a quiet place and have a script of what you are going to say.
2. Open the Voice Recorder app. The following screen will appear:

3. To record, click on the 🎤 button. The following screen will appear:

4. To pause recording, click on the **pause** button.
5. To stop recording, click on the **stop** button. The main screen will reappear:

6. To listen to the recording, select the recording you have just created. It will be at the top left-hand corner of the screen.
7. To delete the recording, right-click on the recording. The following screen will appear:

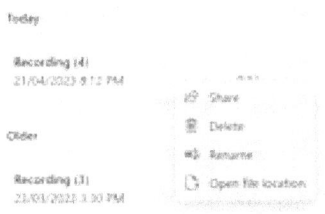

8. Select the **Delete** option.
9. To rename the recording, select **Rename**.

## Prototyping resources

Prototypes or samples can be created using electronic or physical methods. Drawing images initially is a great option, but when appropriate, physical three-dimensional prototypes are useful, particularly when presenting to "clients".

Generally, the creation of prototypes is something that should not increase waste. Reuse of cardboard packaging is ideal, with paints, glue, tape, Plasticine, and air-dried clay being core components.

Maintaining a box or cupboard of commonly used tools and resources is essential to the success of prototyping. However, if an online version is preferred, useful starting points are:

- Adobe Dimension
- Autodesk Fusion 360.

These products are available free for education purposes for one year. Further videos are available from STEAMauthenticity.com. Basic skills development is provided below.

### Adobe Dimension

Adobe Dimension is a 3D mock-up tool which is ideal for showcasing , branding and staging products.

1. Using Adobe Creative Cloud, install Adobe Dimension.
2. Once installed, click on the **Dimension App** button. The following screen will appear:

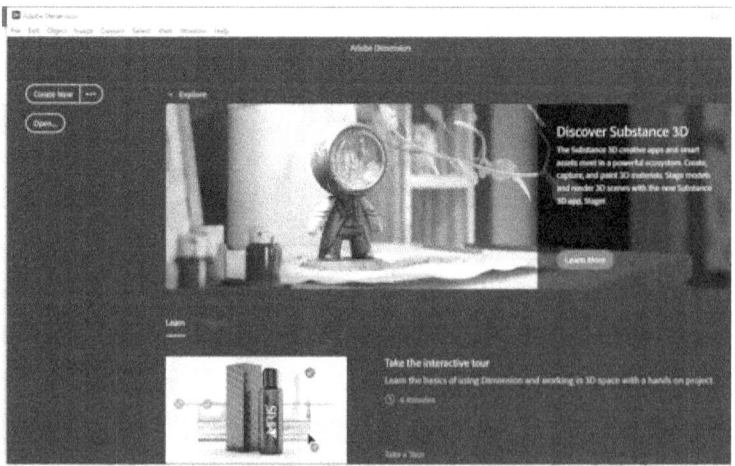

3. Click on **Create New**. The following screen will appear:

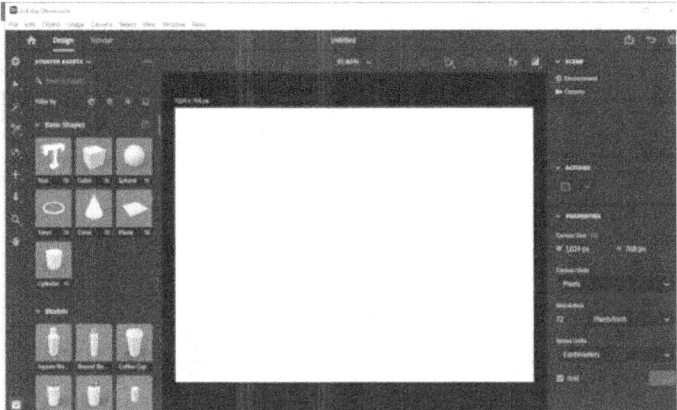

4. To move and select within the Dimension space, there are five main buttons in the left-hand toolbar. These are listed and detailed below:

| Tool | Description |
|---|---|
|   | Allows you to add and import content using the categories below:  Starter Assets, CC Libraries, Import Your Content, Adobe Stock, Browse Substance Source |
|   | The **Select Tool** allows you to select items within the Dimension space to move them. |
|   | The **Orbit Tool** allows the Dimension space to be viewed from different angles |
|   | The **Pan Tool** allows the Dimension space to be viewed up, down, left and right. |
|   | The **Dolly Tool** allows the Dimension space to be viewed closely or from a long distance as if there was a camera on a dolly. |

Virtual and augmented reality   171

5. Starter assets will also appear on the left-hand side and can be turned off and on using the buttons at the top of the asset list.
6. These assets include:

| Asset Type | Description |
|---|---|
| | **Models:** Contains a series of shapes and simple structures to be added to the Dimension space. 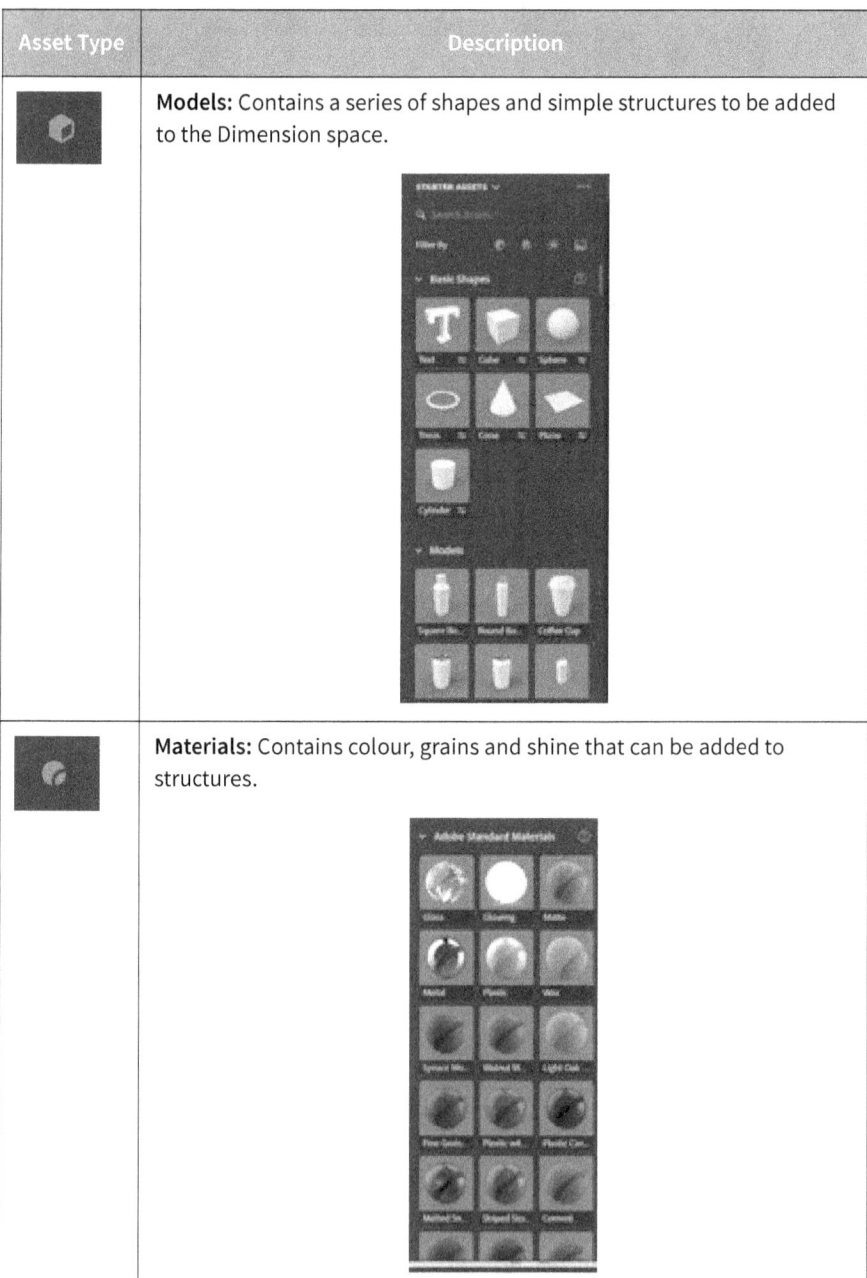 |
| | **Materials:** Contains colour, grains and shine that can be added to structures. |

| Asset Type | Description |
| --- | --- |
|  | **Lights:** Allows different types of light to be added from different directions, for added realism.<br>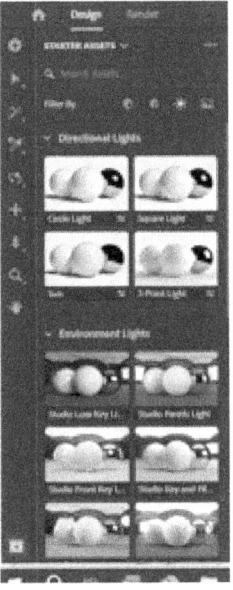 |
|  | **Images:** Allows background images to be added to the Dimension stage as required.<br> |

7. To add items to the Dimension stage, click on the item you wish to add. Use the **Select** tool to select and move. Add structure and detail as required.

Once the image is completed, it will be necessary to use the render menu to fully render the image so that it can be used elsewhere. To access rendering, click on the **Render** menu. The following screen will appear:

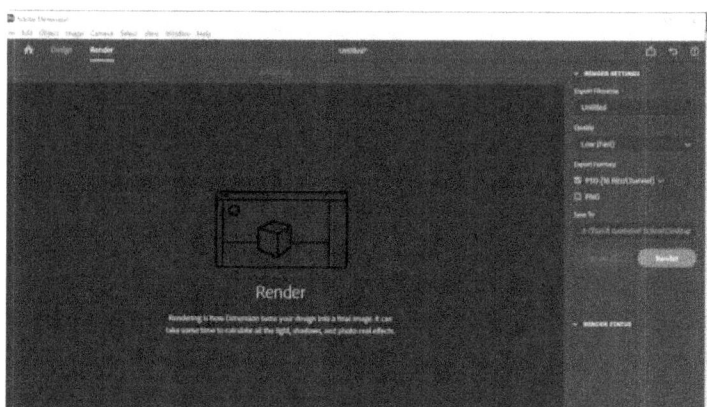

The option is available to create an image in either Photoshop or PNG format. Once the format is chosen, click on the **Render** button. This will take some time to complete.

## Autodesk Fusion 360

Autodesk Fusion is a fantastic tool for creating three-dimensional models that can be used within 3D printing or CNC routing options.

1. Open the Autodesk Fusion 360 app. The following screen will appear:

2. Click on the **Create Sketch** button, then click on the drawing grid section of the screen. The following screen will appear:

3. To create sketches:
   i. Click on the shape you wish to draw with.
   ii. Move your mouse to the screen, click and hold your click, then draw the shape roughly to the size you wish to use:

   iii. To choose an exact value, type in the size you would like. This will change the value in the blue highlighted area. Press **Enter** to lock the value in.
4. Click on the **Finish Sketch** button. The menus will then change back to what is seen below:

5. At the top right-hand side of the screen, you will see the image below:

6. This image is used to adjust the angle or view you can see. This occurs by clicking on the desired side.
7. To make the image three-dimensional, it is possible to use the **Extrude** option. To do this, click on the shape, and it will change to look as below:

8. Click on **Create**. The following menu will appear:

9. Click on the **Extrude** option. The following screen will appear:

10. The extrude option can be completed by clicking on the blue arrow, or by typing a value in the **Distance** box, then clicking on OK.

## ThingLink

ThingLink is an interactive tool that allows you to create digital experiences and use them in a virtual reality environment that can be viewed with virtual reality headsets. Images, text, video, hyperlinks and hotspots can be set up so that users can have an immersive and creative experience that adds to teaching and learning. Content can range from simple to complex, with examples including simple assignment tasks, virtual tours of schools and escape rooms. This is a very versatile product that is free to use, though a more advanced version can be purchased at a minimal cost.

### Setting up login

1. Go to https://www.thinglink.com. Click on **Try for free**. Once you have created a login, click on **Log in**. The following screen will appear:

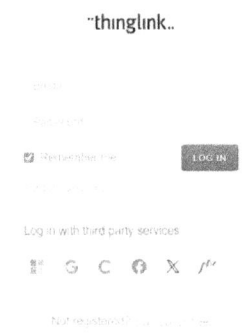

2. Type in your email and password, then click on **Log in**. The following screen will appear:

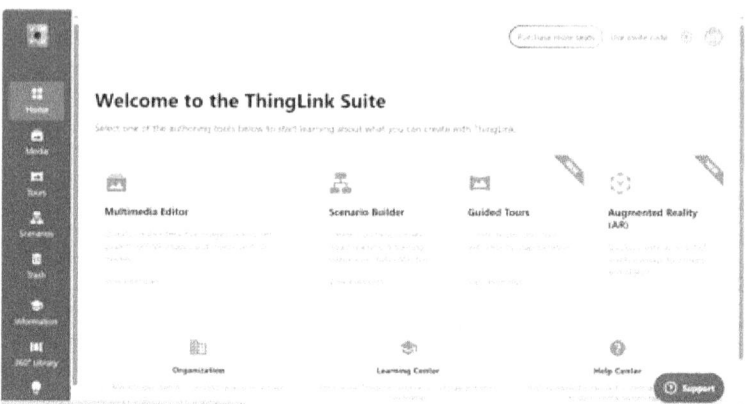

3. Click on the **Media** button. The following screen will appear:

4. When creating content, click on the **Create** button. The following screen will appear:

5. Type in the name of your new folder, then click on the **Create** button. The folder will now be created.

## Adding content

1. To add content, click on the **Create** button. The following screen will appear:

2. Files can be added by dragging them onto the space provided. They will look as shown below:

3. Click on the **Continue** button. The screen will appear as shown below:

4. To begin linking, double-click on the page that will be your cover page. It will look like this:

5. Click on the **Edit** button. The following screen will appear:

## Adding tags

1. To add tags, or connections, click on the **Add tag** button. The following screen will appear:

2. To add content that can be viewed **within a page**, click on the **Text and media** button. The following screen will appear:

3. This page will allow you to change the icon, add a title, a description, and a URL, and upload audio or other media files.
4. To add content that will link to other pages, click on **Transit**. The following screen will appear:

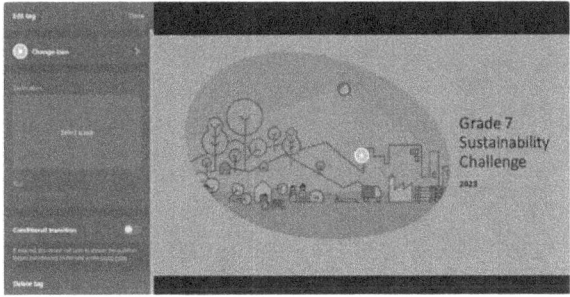

5. Click on **Change icon** to select a different button/icon.
6. Once changed, move the icon to the position on the screen of your choosing.
7. Click on **Select score** to select the scene you wish to link to. The following screen will appear:

Virtual and augmented reality   181

8. Click on the page you would like to link to. The page will now change to what is shown below:

9. The **Conditional transition** allows you to change to different pages, by making the transition dependent on adding a question.
10. If you would like to add a question as a conditional option to get to the next page, it will be necessary to turn on **Conditional transition**. The following screen will appear:

11. Type a question into the **Question** box, then type the correct answer into the **Correct answer** box.
12. If you would like the question to be multiple choice, type the choices into the **Choices** box, separated by a comma. The screen will look like this:

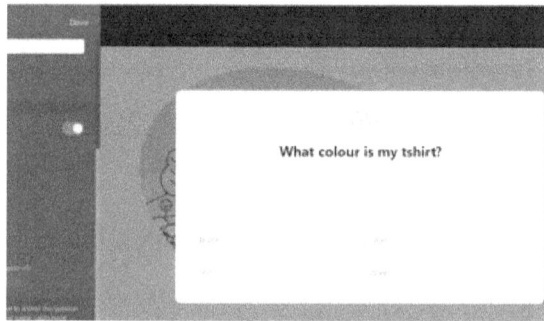

13. Click on **Done** to finish.
14. Repeat as necessary.

Note: The content that is added can be photos, drawn images, PowerPoint slides turned into photos, videos or 360 images.

### Editing tags

1. To make changes to a tag, open the page that contains the tag.
2. Click on the tag you wish to change.
3. Edit as needed by modifying what is within the tag.

### Running the ThingLink

1. Double-click to open the first page of the ThingLink.
2. Click on the link on the first page and continue through the links.

### Sharing the ThingLink

1. Before sharing the ThingLink, it will be necessary to open each page in turn and adjust the privacy settings.
2. Once the page is open, click on the **Privacy settings** button. The following screen will appear:

3. Adjust privacy as needed, then click on the **Save** button.
4. Repeat as necessary.
5. To share, click on the **Share** button. The following screen will then appear:

6. Select the option that you wish to use for sharing.

Note: These options may vary depending on whether you have a free account or a paid account.

Virtual and augmented reality   183

# Building custom apps

There are numerous app builders on the market, many of which are suitable for simple systems. The one described here is App Inventor, which can be accessed at https://www.jotform.com and is wonderful for beginner users.

## Planning your app

Before starting, it is necessary to work out what the app will do and how it will be constructed. This is best done by using a mind map, as described previously, and planning the functionality and linkages of the app.

Think about things like:

- What would the user want?
- How could the app appeal to that user?
- What colours, images, logos and designs fit the type of app you are building?

It is also necessary to make sure that:

- The links work.
- Images are easy to load and see.
- The text is simple, logical and correctly spelt.

## Getting started

1. Visit https://www.jotform.com. The following screen will appear:

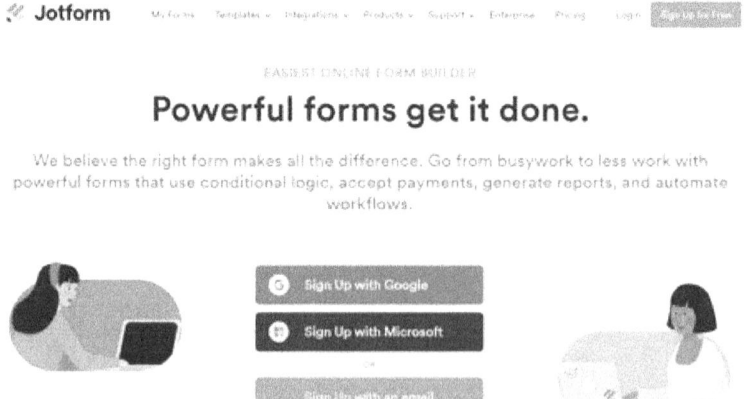

2. If you would like to create a login, click on the **Sign Up for Free** button. The following screen will appear:

3. It is possible to use Jotform without logging in. To do so, click on the **Product** tab. The following screen will appear:

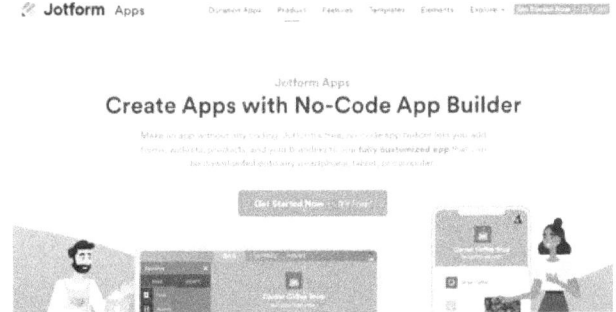

4. Click on **Get Started Now**. The following screen will appear:

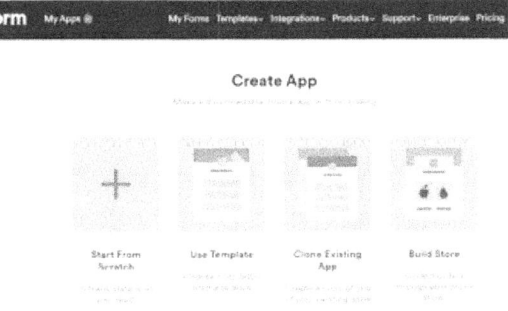

5. Click on **+ Start From Scatch**. The following screen will appear:

6. Type in the name of the app in the **App Name** box.
7. To change the icon, click on **Edit Icon**. The following screen will appear:

8. Change the image by clicking on the **Image**, or alternatively select the **Icon** button to select and adjust the colour and style of the icon.

186   Creating Authenticity in STEAM Education

9. Click on the **Back** button when completed. The following screen will appear:

10. Click on the **Done** button. The following screen will appear:

11. To change the app title, click on **App Title**. The following screen will appear:

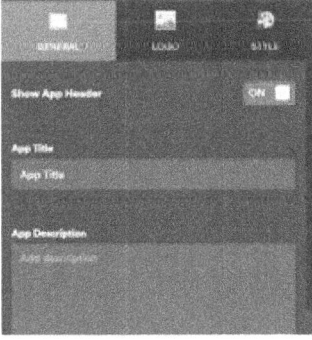

12. Change details as required and then click on the **X**.

## Adding elements

1. To begin adding elements to your app, click on **Add Elements**. The following screen will appear:

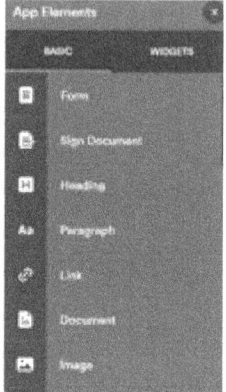

2. Add elements to your page by clicking on the required element and dragging it to the following area:

3. If adding a heading, it will appear as follows:

4. To delete an element, click on the 🗑.
5. In the **Basic** tab, repeat for the following main element types:
   a. Heading
   b. Paragraph
   c. Link
   d. Image
   e. Button
   f. Product list
   g. Image gallery

6. In the **Widgets** tab, the following screen will appear:

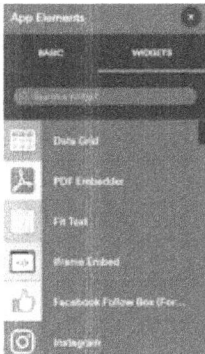

## Adding pages

1. To add a page to your app, click on the **+ Add a Page** option. The following screen will appear:

2. Continue to add pages as required, adding elements to each page using your app plan as a guide.

## Linking pages

1. Buttons can be used to link to pages. See the link below:

Virtual and augmented reality 189

2. To link the page, click on **Button**. The following screen will appear:

3. To adjust settings, click on the ✽ button. The following screen will appear:

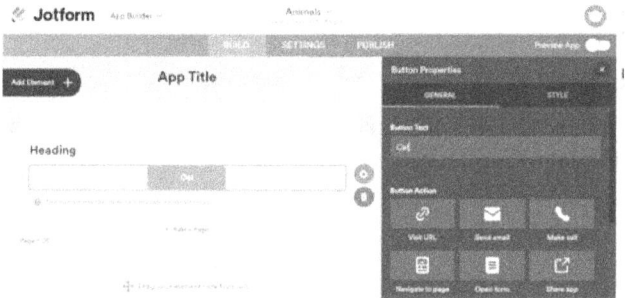

4. Change **Button Text** to the appropriate name.
5. Set the **Button Action** to what you would like the button link to do. Options include:
   a. Visit URL
   b. Send email
   c. Navigate to page, and so on.
6. To link pages, Click on **Navigate to page**.
7. Below this button, the following screen will appear:

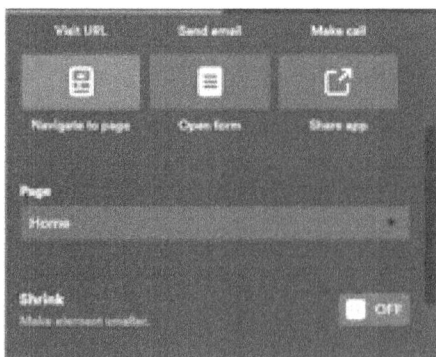

8. Click on the drop-down arrow to the right of the **Home** option and select the appropriate page. Repeat, as necessary.

## Previewing app

1. To preview the app, click on **Preview App**. The screen will then appear as below:

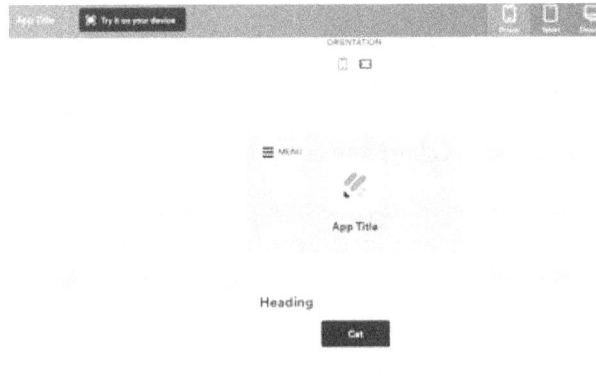

2. To change the orientation of the app, click on **Orientation**.
3. To see how the app would look on different devices, click on **Phone | Tablet | Desktop**.
4. To try it on your own device, click on **Try it on your device**. The following screen will appear:

5. It is possible to download, use a QR code, or copy a link as needed.

Virtual and augmented reality   191

CHAPTER 19

# General skills

## Logos, symbols and mascots

Logos, symbols and mascots are essential components of the STEAM Framework, with a particular focus within the art element. Visualising the look for the product or process helps to create an overarching view of what has been created.

This overarching view of what needs to be produced can also extend to document creation to create a visually pleasing effect. Why is this important? Regardless of whether the client or viewer notices the visual aspect, the overall impression will be there. While there are many products that can meet the needs of creating logos, icons and mascots, Word and Canva are two of the simplest, and allow for the most creativity. While drawing and conceptualising mascots is fun if you feel capable of doing so, Midjourney and Discord allow those who feel that they are less artistic to develop something creative with the use of artificial intelligence.

Some of the concepts to be covered are:

- Simple Microsoft Word style guide
- Introduction to Canva
- Introduction to Discord and Midjourney.

## Word style guide

Word documentation could make up a large component of this book, but this guide focuses directly on skills that will be important for making presentations, advertisements and documentation for STEAM challenges.

## Adding styles to text

In documents meant for advertising and presentation it is essential that all fonts, colours and designs meet the needs of the style guide. Styles are available from the **Styles** section on the **Home** tab. Styles are set up in basic formats as below:

These styles can be modified to suit the requirements of the document.

1. Type in the content you wish to use for your heading.
2. Click somewhere within the heading, and from the **Styles** button select the heading option you wish to use – for example **Heading 1**.
3. Repeat as necessary, keeping in mind that:
   - Heading 1 is a main heading.
   - Heading 2 is a subheading.
   - Heading 3 is a sub-subheading.
   - Normal is the standard text for the Word document.

## Changing the way styles look

1. Highlight the text with the style you want to change. The following screen will appear:

2. Change the font, size, colour and alignment of the text to its new formatting.

3. Click on **Styles**. The following screen will appear:

4. Right-click on the style of the text you have highlighted. The following screen will appear:

5. Select **Update Heading 3 to Match Selection**. This will change all the content that is formatted in that style to match the changes made to what has been highlighted.

## Introduction to tables

Tables are an excellent way to format information into clear columns, and are also a wonderful way to align pictures and headings, as well as create forms. The basics for this are shown below.

1. From the **Insert** menu, select **Table**. The following screen will appear:

2. Select the correct number of columns. It isn't necessary to select the correct number of rows, because if you run out of rows, you only have to press the Tab key and a new row will appear.
3. Once the table has been created, use the Tab key to move forward in the table, and Shift + Tab to move backward in the table.

## To merge cells

1. To merge cells, select two or more cells in the table and right-click. The following menu will appear:

2. Click on the **Merge Cells** button.

## Adding and deleting rows and columns

1. Columns and rows are easily created. Move your mouse to where you would like to add your column or row. A "plus" sign will appear:

2. Click on the plus sign, and a new column will be created.

# Canva

## Creating a login

1. Go to https://www.canva.com. The following screen will appear:

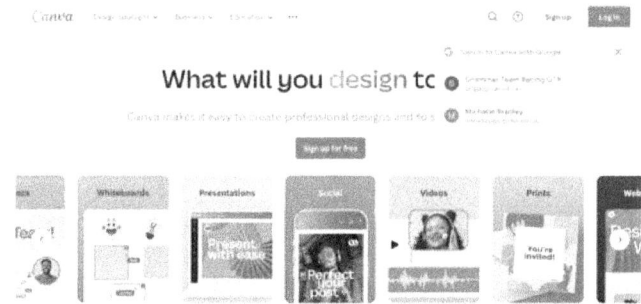

2. Click on the **Sign up** button. The following screen will appear:

3. Create a login with one of the suggested formats.
4. Once the login has been created, the following screen will appear:

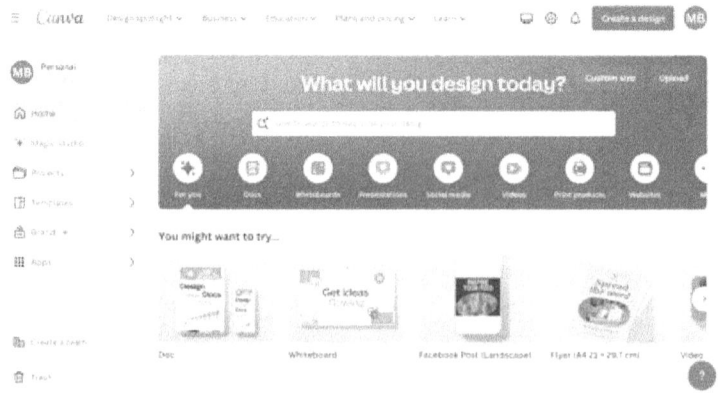

## Creating designs and custom images

1. To create some standard-sized designs, click on **Create a design**. The following screen will appear:

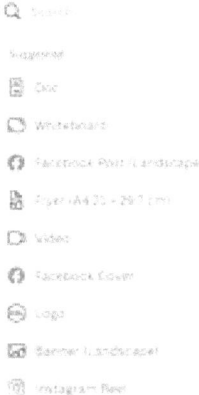

2. Select the type of design you wish to use, then begin designing.
3. To create a customised image, click on **Custom size**. The following screen will appear:

4. Generally:
   - Banners are around 1600 x 200 pixels.
   - Buttons are around 300 x 300 pixels.

## Creating images

1. Once your image size has been selected (in this case it is a banner), the following screen will appear:

2. To add images:
   - Copy and paste either from your own selection or from a search engine, or
   - Use one of the templates and styles at the left-hand side of the screen.
3. To resize images, click on the item you wish to resize, as shown below:

Click on one of the circles at the corner of the image or text box and drag in or out as needed.

4. To delete items, click on the item you wish to delete, then press the Delete key on your keyboard.

## Changing colours

1. Click on the element on the screen you wish to change.
2. At the top left-hand corner of the screen, click on the colour option: ■.

3. The following menu will appear:

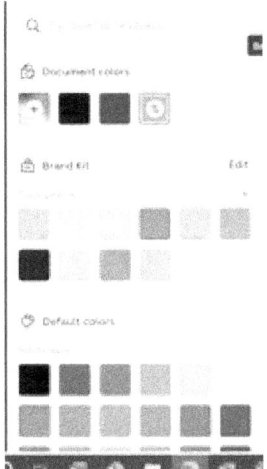

4. Select the colour you wish to adjust, then repeat as necessary.

## Adding text

Click on **Text** to add text, then adjust size and colour as required.

## Copying images

Once a button or image has been created, it is possible to copy elements using the **+** button.

## Downloading images

1. To download an image, click on the **Share** button. The following screen will appear:

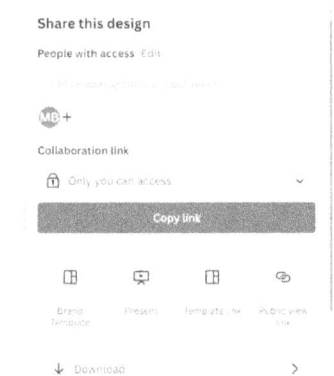

2. Click the **Download** button. The following screen will appear:

3. Click on **Download**, then retrieve the item from the Downloads folder on your computer.

## Creating animations

1. Click on the **Animate** button. The following screen will appear:

2. Click on the animation option. The following screen will appear:

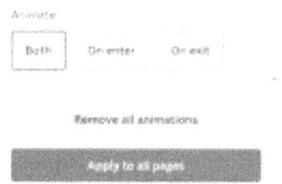

3. This will allow you to change animations on exit and on enter, or to remove all animations.

# Excel introduction

Below are instructions for most areas of Excel. They are given as a reference for use during class time or during assessment.

Some basic points:

1. There are 256 columns and 66,536 rows in each sheet, and multiple sheets can be used (up to 39 effectively, but more can be added).
2. Columns can be adjusted by dragging the vertical line to the right of the column, but a better way is to move your mouse to the same position and double-click. This adjusts the column automatically to the width of the widest column.
3. Most formatting is the same as in Word (e.g. bold, italics, alignment). The following are the main areas that are different:

    - Merging cells – found in **Format**, **Cells**, **Alignment**, **Merge Cells**
    - Wrap text – found in **Format**, **Cells**, **Alignment**, **Wrap Text**

    Using tool bar buttons, details are shown below:

    | Icon | Description |
    |---|---|
    |  | Merge and centre – highlight multiple cells and click this button |
    |  | Currency |
    |  | Percentage |
    |  | Comma style – not generally used, it puts commas after thousands |
    |  | Increase decimal – increases the number of decimal places in the cell |
    |  | Decrease decimal – decreases the number of decimal places in the cell |
    |  | Decrease indent – decreases indent within cell |
    |  | Increase indent– allows you to indent the values within the cell instead of adding spaces |
    |  | Borders – adds borders in, which can also be done through **Format**, . **Cells**, but this is quicker. |

4. **Naming sheets** – it is important to name sheets rather than leave them as Sheet 1 etc.

## Formula creation

1. Always start a formula with an equals (=) sign.
2. Rather than typing in cell references, click on the cells you want to use in your formula, and they will automatically be added (this helps with logical thinking).
3. Operators are as follows:
   a. Addition is +
   b. Subtraction is –
   c. Multiplication is *
   d. Division is /
   e. The same BODMAS rules apply with brackets within Excel as in mathematics.
4. To fill formulas across click on the **Autofill** notch (this is the black square at the bottom right-hand corner of the cell) and then drag across to the desired cell. To fill formulas down use the same method, but it is also possible to double-click if there is information in the column to the left of the one you are working in.

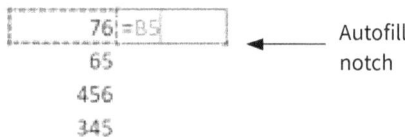

Autofill notch

## Absolute cell referencing

Sometimes when a formula is filled down, an error occurs. This is usually because part of the formula needs to reference a particular cell for *all* the formulaes. This is done by locking the formula into that cell using absolute cell referencing.

To do this, use dollar ($) signs on the cells you want to lock. There are a variety of ways that this can be done:

| Locking method | Result |
| --- | --- |
| $B4 | Locks the formula into **just** the column |
| B$4 | Locks the formula into **just** the row |
| $B$4 | Locks the formula into **both** column and row |

The disadvantage of using absolute cell referencing is that $B$4 doesn't mean anything to someone when they are further down the sheet. It is better to name the cells. This is discussed in the next section.

## Naming cells and ranges

Naming cells and ranges when creating formulas allows you to:

- Create meaningful formulas – for example: = CostPrice*NumberSold
- It also means that the named cell is available and understood on any sheet within the workbook.

To create a named cell:

1. Click on the cell (or select the range) you want to name.
2. Click in the **Name** box in the top left-hand corner of the screen:

3. Type in the name of the cell or range (remember no spaces – underscores and upper and lower case are fine).
4. Press **Enter**. This is the most important step, as it won't name the cell or range otherwise.

That cell or range is now available anywhere on the worksheet.

**Note:** Naming ranges is particularly useful when using the VLOOKUP function.

## Auto sum button

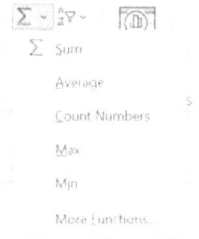

The Auto Sum button is by far the easiest way to create basic totals. This can be done by:

General skills 203

1. Clicking where the answer is to go
2. Clicking on the Auto Sum button: Σ
3. Pressing **Enter** if the area highlighted is correct (dotted lines indicate which cells are going to be added up; if this area is incorrect, just re-select the correct cells).

### Minimum, maximum and average

1. Use the same method: click on the drop-down arrow to the right of the Auto Sum button and select the appropriate function.
2. It is also possible to click on **More Functions** under the Auto Sum button to access all the other available functions.
3. Another method to access this Function Wizard is to click on the *fx* button to the left of the formula bar. If you click on it, the following dialog will appear:

4. It is then possible to select a category (as shown with the drop-down).

### VLookup

This is a useful function as it allows you to "look up" values in a vertical table, hence the name. There is also an equivalent **Hlookup** allowing you to look up values in a vertical table.

1. Before starting, it is useful to access or type in the table of information that you require. For example, if creating a lookup table to allocate grades to percentages for a given test, the table might be similar to below:

| A | 85% |
| B | 65% |
| C | 48% |
| D | 30% |
| E | 10% |

This table would mean that 85% and above would be an A, between 65% and 84% would be a B and so on.
2. This second step is not necessary but makes for a better formula.
   a. Highlight the table.
   b. Name the table (see above section).
3. Click on the **More Functions** button and select VLOOKUP. Click on OK. The following dialog will appear:

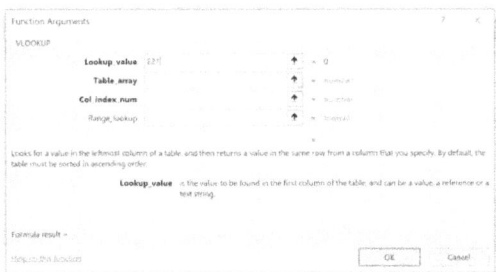

4. Type in **Lookup_value** – this is the value you are looking for.
5. Type in the **Table_array** – this is where the value is stored (your named range).
6. Type in the **Col_index_num** – this is the column in your named range that the answer can be found in.
7. If required, type in the **Range_lookup**. To find the closest match to the value, type in TRUE; otherwise type in FALSE.

Note: It is essential that the first column is in ascending order (whether it is alpha or numeric).

## *If statements*

If statements are useful if you want to use different values or type in different words depending on the contents of another cell or other cells.

1. Click on the **More Functions** button, and select If. The following dialog will appear:

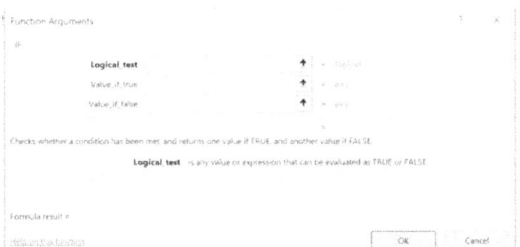

2. Type in the **Logical_test**. This is the thing that you are testing – e.g. if A2<6.
3. Type in the **Value_if_true**. This is what you want to appear in the cell if the logical test is met. It can be a formula, cell reference, number or text value. If it is a text value, then place double quotes around the value.
4. Type in the **Value_if_false**. This is the value that you want to appear if the logical test is false. The same rules apply as in point 3.
5. Click on **OK**.

Note: It is possible to have "nested" if statements. This allows you to have loops within loops of IF statements.

## Paste special

Sometimes copying and pasting does not work as required, as formulas and/or formatting are transferred when you do not want them to be. To avoid this, try the following:

1. Copy as required.
2. Right-click on the cell you want to paste into. The following dialog box will appear:

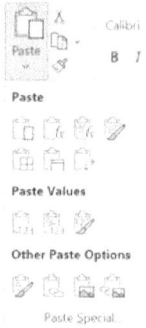

3. Select the **Paste Special** button. The following screen will appear:

Select one of the following (these are the most likely to be used):
a. **Values** (just copies over numbers, no formatting or formulas)
b. **Values and number formats** (copies numbers and formats, but not formulas)
c. **Transpose** (allows you to change values from a vertical list to a horizontal list and vice versa).

## Data validation

Data validation allows you to check that the values within cells have been entered correctly, and allows you to have input and error messages in place.

1. From the Data menu, select **Data Tools**. The following dialog will appear:

2. Click on **Data Validation**. The following screen will appear:

3. In the **Allow** tab, the drop-down contains:

4. Selecting Whole Number allows you to specify a whole number and then determine a range that the whole number will be within. Decimal, Date, Time and Text Length are similar.

5. The exception and one of the most useful options is **List**. This will allow you to create an in-cell drop-down list. When you select this from the list, the following dialog will appear:

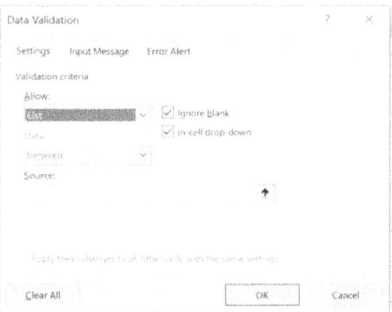

6. Under **Source**, type in the values you would like to appear in your drop-down list, separated by commas.
7. Click on **OK**. The drop-down list is now fully usable, and will allow only those values to be entered in the cells.

### Sorting

Sorting is essential for many of the elements that I will be looking at next. Some basic points about sorting are:

1. Sorting can be found in the **Data** menu, under **Sort**.
2. It is not necessary to highlight the whole area to sort. It is just necessary to click somewhere in the list.

## Intermediate Excel

### AutoFilter

This allows large data sets to be filtered.

**To turn AutoFilter on**

Note: AutoFilter can be left on at all times, even when refreshing the data. If you would prefer to leave it on, it will not affect any functionality.

From the **Data** menu, select **Filter**, then **AutoFilter**.

**To turn off AutoFilter**

From the **Data** menu, select **Filter**.

## To filter on an item in the list

1. To filter, for example, on one heading, click on the drop-down arrow to the right of the top cell in the column. The following menu will appear:

## *Looking for blanks or non-blanks*

Sometimes it is handy to look for people who *don't* have information in their field.

Example: People whose email address we don't have.

1. Click on the drop-down arrow to the right of the **Email** heading.
2. Scroll to the very bottom of the list.
3. Select blanks.

The same can apply for non-blanks. This could be used to find people who *do* have a value in a certain column.

## *Subtotals*

Subtotals are very useful, but it is *essential* that the list is sorted on whatever the subtotals are being created on (e.g. gender).

### Creating subtotals

1. From the **Data** menu, select **Outline**. The following dialog will appear:

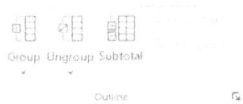

2. Click on the **Subtotal** option. The following screen will appear:

   a. **At each change in** means "every time there is a change in..." e.g. name.
   b. **Use function** allows you to select **Sum** or **Count**, etc.
   c. **Add subtotal to** allows you to add the answer under a certain column.
   d. **Replace current subtotals** means get rid of any subtotals used before. It is also possible to untick this box and leave in any subtotals.
   e. If you are working with groups, e.g. grade, it is possible to use **Page break between groups**.
3. Click on **OK**.

**Removing subtotals**
1. From the Data menu, select **Outline** and then **Subtotal**.
2. Click on the **Remove all** button.

**Using subtotals**
Once subtotals have been created, a strip will appear to the left of the cells:

1. Use **1** if you would like to just see the **Grand Total**.
2. Use **2** if you want to see the **Subtotal Values**.
3. Use **3** if you want to see all the information.
4. To expand just one subtotal, click on any **+** button.
5. To minimise any given subtotal, click on any **-** button.

210  Creating Authenticity in STEAM Education

# PART 6
# DEVELOPING AUTHENTICITY ACROSS THE CURRICULUM

"If you want to build a ship, do not drum up the men to gather wood, divide the work and give orders. Instead, teach them to yearn for the vast and endless sea."

– ANTOINE DE SAINT-EXUPÉRY (1900–1944)

CHAPTER 20

# Beginning integration of STEAM learning

The integration of the Authentic STEAM Framework is not something that can be developed in a short space of time, but each stage of implementation will have educational value and will be a major step in the right direction.

Modelling best practice and beginning incorporation into areas such as science, design and digital technology is a great place to begin. This will allow concepts to be trialled and some adjustments of process to be made to enable assimilation into an educational landscape. However, a whole-school approach to the development of key skills, understandings and capabilities is a key requirement to ensure long-term transfer.

## Deciding on your school's STEAM approach

It is important to have a plan before beginning. This can take many forms but should be detailed with entry points and measurable milestones. Before beginning your STEAM program, it is useful to look at what your various milestones are and what the outcomes of those milestones should be. Initially, this should be determined by a whole-school plan – a map that will determine what a successful STEAM program looks like. Bertolini (2022) confirms that this approach is effective "with the aim of conveying how a school is bringing curriculum, capabilities and learning together as a cohesive whole".

An approach that enhances the implementation of a whole-school program is to look at the end point or success criteria that you wish to develop – the characteristics, experiences and understandings that a student graduating from your school should possess. Some of these success criteria may include, but not be limited to:

- Using computational thinking and design thinking skills to break down problems and produce solutions
- Saying "Yes" to challenges, with the knowledge that the student can find a way to complete what is needed
- Being a creative thinker who can think outside the box to seek solutions
- Being intrinsically motivated – not requiring outside input to perform effectively
- Being mindful of their own wellbeing and the wellbeing of others, with strategies to support this mindfulness
- Being motivated to support their own community and those further afield.

> One of the best parts of being a teacher is one that is not talked about every day. It is that moment when a student understands a concept or develops a strategy that you have supported them in. To see a student succeed and go beyond what they thought they were capable of is the most amazing feeling, and one that keeps me going. The characteristics listed above are the ones I strive for every time.

## Relationships, relationships, relationships

Educators understand the importance of building relationships as an essential component of effective teaching. It is and should be the beginning, middle and end of your experience with each student, and with your fellow educators. Some relationships come easily; others do not. But over time it has become obvious that to teach a student effectively, you must know who they are, how they work, and what they need to succeed.

Using the Authentic STEAM Framework is a great way to allow educators to build and maintain these relationships. Students feel seen, heard and understood, and find it easier to shine within this format than within a traditional teacher-led format.

> Magic Johnson once said, "All kids need is a little hope, a little help, and someone who believes in them". Your relationship with your students is the key to a successful STEAM education program, and to your success as an educator. Every child needs a new slate – some every day, some every term.

Your belief in the possibility of who they are shapes them. So even when it is hard, find the kernel of good.

## Creating student agency

Student agency is the requirement for students to have control over their own learning and presents opportunities for students to "learn how to learn". In other words, the process of learning and skill development is just as important as the result that is achieved. Our world is changing so quickly that it will be essential for our students to be able to learn, unlearn and learn again, to adapt to ever-changing work and personal environments with passion and excitement, not fear.

Students who feel that they have a voice, and a measure of control over their personal and educational landscape, will be much more adaptable than others who are not given those same opportunities. Students who "play an active role in deciding what and how they will learn… tend to show greater motivation to learn and are more likely to define objectives for their learning" (OECD, 2019).

Research for this book has led down many and various paths, some amazing, some limiting. A lot of existing STEAM programs and challenges have not given much scope for student agency. The challenges are great, but instead of asking students to solve problems, they state the problem and then give them specific ways to respond, or instructions on how to create projects.

The most authentic learning and the best intrinsic motivation comes from the pride and ownership a student takes from these STEAM experiences.

> At the start of every year, I say to my Grade 10 to 12 students that the gift or curse I will give them is the inability to enter any business or work environment without being able to analyse issues, simplify workflows or start problem-solving.
>
> This is something I live with myself because of previous lessons in problem-solving. They all smile at me, clearly not believing me. But sooner or later, one or more will tell me, "You won't believe what happened on the weekend…" The story will not be about something they have done, but a business they have visited which is working in an inefficient way.
>
> This is what student agency and the development of problem-solving ability produces, and it thrills me every time.

## First steps

Begin small, as an addition to existing practice. Traditional formats of teacher-led content followed by an assignment and/or test have worked well for many students in the past, but why not experiment with a different way? If teaching Grade 8 science, and discussing plate tectonics and earthquake-proof building, a great alternative to a test is for students to design and build a simple earthquake-proof building. This design would take around 20 minutes for design and around two lessons to build and trial various iterations. This is a great way to dip your toes in the STEAM challenge waters.

> **Example challenge**
>
> How can we create an earthquake-proof structure that will survive the best in a simulated earthquake environment?
>
> Your team has been asked by an organisation that manages projects for countries in need to design a building that can withstand an earthquake.
>
> Working as structural engineers, you will design, build and test a structure that can withstand an earthquake simulated by a shaker table. You will need to work within this budget:
>
> Materials and equipment:
>
> - Toothpicks ($0.30 each)
> - Skewers ($1.00 each)
> - Plasticine ($1.00 per stick)
> - Scissors.

## Many hands make light work

Before beginning, gather several like-minded educators with a passion for developing content. It is easier to have many hands working together to design, trial and develop content and resources that will work for you all. This can be within your teaching area, or across curriculum areas. The key is not to work in a silo, but to use many hands to make light work.

Once that process has started, working with a small team who are supportive of the process is essential. Getting started in the incorporation of STEAM education is essential to the success of STEAM education within a school.

Working collaboratively is key to successfully integrating the Authentic STEAM Framework across a school. Work together and identify some key areas that the program would fit. From there, develop tasks and challenges together. A rising tide floats all boats, so adding opinions, suggestions and support from your teammates will only enhance and improve the teaching and learning experience for all involved. It is not essential for these colleagues to be mathematics, science or technology educators. Sometimes the greatest ideas come from someone seeing "outside the box" and viewing what is needed in a different way. This can also allow cross-curricular enhancements that will make for better educational experiences and deeper student learning.

## Summary of key points

- Meet with enthusiastic colleagues in relevant subjects.
- Agree on the "language" you are going to use as a team.
- Create visibility of the chosen format through posters and templates.
- Support each other in the development of coursework, tasks and assessments that support the framework.

## Consistency of language

Before incorporation into classes, it is essential that the framework and plan for future learning is agreed upon by all stakeholders. Throughout this book, three different levels of the Authentic STEAM Framework have been discussed:

1. The full Authentic STEAM Framework
2. The Simplified STEAM Framework
3. The Primary-based Authentic STEAM Framework.

While the detail is different, the structure and outcomes are the same. The way that these are implemented within your school will depend on the age(s) of your cohort and the time allocated to support of this program.

This starts with all educators agreeing on a defined language when approaching STEAM and design challenges. This can be discussed as a team, and supported through posters, explanations and templates being shared throughout the necessary teaching and learning areas.

Design technology (wood, metal, food, textile), digital technology, object design, and science all have a similar "language" around problem-solving and design, so are great places to begin incorporation. Student-directed inquiries and other subjects – such as agricultural science – will also work well with this approach.

## The Authentic STEAM Framework

This full framework is used for larger projects – between three double lessons and five days depending on the complexity of the response required. The focus for this framework is generally middle school and older and can be used for grade challenges. Details of what is needed within each of these steps can be found in **Part 2: The Authentic STEAM Framework**.

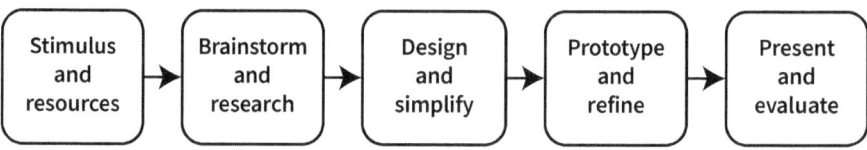

## The Simplified STEAM Framework

The Simplified STEAM Framework is used for tasks that might work within one to four double lessons and can be used from around Grade 1 through to Grade 12. This framework is less detailed, hence tasks can be completed in shorter timeframes or given to younger students. Free downloads of posters are available on the STEAMauthenticity.com website.

While the framework is simplified from the Authentic STEAM Framework, it is basically structured the same, and each section is mapped back to the original. It is not realistic to create larger studies on a regular basis. However, this simplified framework will give a more consistent and continuous approach to the development of STEAM and the design thinking process.

Changes do not need to happen overnight, but a consistent application of this approach to education will gradually develop STEAM within your school until it becomes an innate part of what it does.

The Simplified STEAM Framework holds all the components of the full framework but allows responses using a cut-down approach to learning. The focus is still on user-centred design – in other words, creating for a target customer – but requires faster and shorter responses than the full STEAM Framework.

The components are:

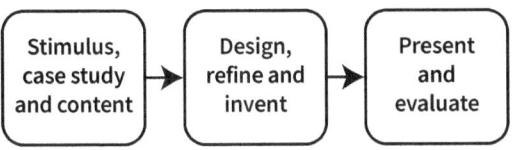

Within each section, students will carry out the following tasks:

## *Stimulus, case study and content*

Tasks are framed with an initial quote, short video, or scripted case study to help students begin thinking around the challenge. Generally, this challenge would be placed at the middle or end of a course of work, as a consolidation or reinforcement of topics covered. Alternatively, though, it could be used in a flipped format as a challenge to develop skills and understanding before delving deeper into content.

In this simplified format, rather than students deciding on a target customer from scratch, the basic components of the target customer are often the focus of the case study. This helps to streamline the process, though some of the fleshing out of the target customer will continue in the next section.

Within this first component, there will also be research options and questions to consider. This will allow the student or groups of students to have a clear understanding of what could be required before continuing.

## *Define, refine and invent*

A deep dive into the target customer and their needs is the focus of this component. The students will then focus on the design process, which will include:

- The discussion of a variety of solutions for completion
- The refinement of the process into more specific terms
- The invention of sample prototypes or processes that solve the problem.

This can take place electronically or on paper, depending on which works best for the students. It is important in this phase that students keep track of their designs, their discussion about those designs, and the refinement and elimination process. These can be documented in a booklet or document, or within a journal.

The process is far more important than the destination, as this is what helps define our progress and enhance our design ability.

## *Present and evaluate*

Presentation will differ depending on the task at hand. Because a number of students suffer from anxiety and fear of speaking in public, it is ideal to give some options. Presentation might mean:

- Display of the final product with explanatory notes attached
- Presentation to a large group in person or via video
- Presentation via "Final Pitch" style product video
- Presentation to a small group or to the individual
- Presentation via written format.

All the above methods work well – either on their own or in combination with one another. Students should be given a choice about how they present content, rather than being told how they *must* present. However, the Authentic STEAM Framework approach does develop the ability to increase courage and skills in small increments. With continuous use of this approach, there should be an improvement in confidence that will spill over into other areas of students' lives.

> In the past 25 years I have worked as a trainer and presenter, with many varied audiences – from 1 person to a classroom of 25 to groups of around 150 people. I love it, and I thrive on the challenge of presenting in a way that is vibrant and entertaining.
>
> However, I still remember being in Grade 8 art and standing in front of a classroom and having a literal panic attack because students were looking at and drawing me. Sometimes in various situations I am still that person.
>
> People rarely believe in my former lack of confidence and the anxiety that still hits me at odd moments.
>
> That is why:
> - I will not force students to present to a whole class unless or until they are ready to do so.
> - I prefer the facilitator approach rather than calling on individuals to answer in a group setting.
> - I build relationships and confidence slowly.
> - My approach is geared to what the students need, at the time that they need it, in the way that they need it.

That Grade 8 girl is why I work the way that I do. Confidence can be built, and STEAM challenges can help with that building process. We just need to trust the process. The results are worth the change in approach.

## The Primary-based Authentic STEAM Framework

This framework is shown below:

The Primary-based Authentic STEAM Framework follows the two previous formats but frames the content in question-based components. This allows simplification of the process to be used not only in STEAM-based tasks but also in other challenge-based tasks.

Flow-on content is important to the effective delivery of these programs and processes. While the question-based options are very simplified, and the tasks they surround not as detailed, there is still the scope to develop meaningful learning in simplified ways.

The focus within the Primary-based Authentic STEAM Framework may require more educator intervention, depending on the age and experience of the students. However, there is still the ability to develop students' problem-solving and design thinking skills and for them to gain confidence in the presentation of their responses.

The other advantage, particularly in a K to 12 school, is that by developing these required skills at an early age, the transition to more detailed and complex tasks and frameworks is not as difficult. Students understand the process, recognise the skills, and can adjust accordingly.

Within each section, students will need to carry out tasks within the following clear categories:

### *What is our challenge?*

Students are given a challenge and need to understand what they are being asked. This may be a task such as "Develop an understanding of how objects move". Equally, it could be "How can we encourage children to have screen-free time?"

The second option is indicative of a strategy that I regularly use. Instead of focusing, for example, on "We want you to get off your computers/phones, so how can we do that?" I flip the focus. Changing the focus to look at another group (someone other than them) encourages them to solve the problem and seek strategies for themselves without realising they are doing so. Once the task is complete, the reflection process allows them to see that the skills and information could be applied in their situation as well.

Sneaky, but effective!

### How can we find out about it?

This component of the process will contain "Questions to consider" and short videos or relevant links that focus learning to bring out a viable end point. Further research and questioning are encouraged before the design process is started. Group work is encouraged, as a way to streamline the research process and begin the conversation around finding successful solutions to the problems.

### How can we design our solution?

The design process in this framework would be mostly paper-based but could use electronic formats if needed or desired. Minecraft, for example, is a great tool if managed correctly. Students are often able to collaboratively produce designs quickly and effectively within Minecraft – from tiny homes to models of body systems. While there are other tools for creating 3D models, Minecraft is much faster than any of them.

Students need to be encouraged to design multiple options within their group (whether paper-based or electronic) and be able to discuss the pros and cons of each concept. Once this has happened, as a group they will be able to refine their concepts into a more cohesive whole.

### What can we create?

Depending on the task, this may be a basic process comprising one or two options on paper or a detailed, three-dimensional prototype or concept. Cardboard is your friend in this process or other single-use products that have been discarded. Drawing, painting and creating bring the concept to life and make it real.

This part of the process is important in two main ways:

- Students who need to move, build and create can be encouraged to participate and problem-solve through a physical design process.
- This is where the "A" for Art in STEAM comes in. Combining the design process with creativity allows students to feel more engaged and part of the process at hand.

## *How can we show our learning?*

Once again choice is key and should vary depending on the task. Sharing the design process and the outcome is also an important part of encouraging students to learn. Their questions to each other are also essential:

- What is the best thing about your design?
- What do you still have questions about?
- How does this solve the problem?

All these questions and any others they have need to be asked with respect and understanding. The process and the development of skills are what is important – more so than the final product.

## Mapping the three frameworks

Below is a table showing the detail of how the three frameworks work together. This is essential when looking at a full-school approach to STEAM education and allows a clear path for the development of skills and concepts within any burgeoning program.

| The Authentic STEAM Framework | | | | |
|---|---|---|---|---|
| Stimulus and resources | Brainstorm and research | Design and simplify | Prototype and refine | Present and evaluate |
| The Simplified STEAM Framework | | | | |
| Stimulus, case study and content | | Design, refine and invent | | Present and evaluate |
| The Primary-based STEAM Framework | | | | |
| What is our challenge? | How can we find out about it? | How can we design a solution? | What can we create? | How can we show our learning? |

As you will see, all components map in a way that shows a clear process and clarity of design. Obviously not all schools go from kindergarten to Year 12, but this framework is part of an ongoing development of skills that will enable students to prepare themselves for the way they want to work and the life they want to live.

## The importance of microlearnings

An essential component of each of the three frameworks is the use of microlearnings. Microlearnings are small learning components that meet the needs of the student where they are, with what they know and what they need to understand. They are designed for short and sharp concept and skill development, on an as-needed basis.

Many microlearning concepts have been included in this book. At STEAMauthenticity.com, each of these microlearnings will be made available for use in video format.

Microlearnings have many advantages, but three in particular stand out:

1. If students already have the necessary understanding to complete a challenge, they do not need to complete the microlearnings to complete the task.
2. If a student does not have the required skills or understanding, the microlearnings give the student the ability to quickly understand the concept and move on to successful completion of the task.
3. For educators, if a challenge is new, the microlearnings provide a quick way to build skills and understand what is needed before the task begins.

Generally, the microlearnings are essential to completing tasks and challenges quickly and effectively, without having to wait for others to begin or catch up.

Ensuring the availability of appropriate microlearnings in either printed or online format is essential for the success of the Authentic STEAM Framework. Having these learnings easily and logically available to staff and students allows personalised learning. This is only used if needed and can be revisited easily.

Depending on the background and experience of the students completing the task, the amount of scaffolding provided through microlearning may vary. For the initial tasks, microlearnings required to complete the task are identified within the task document. As time progresses, however, the microlearnings may be placed in a central location, and students and educators alike should be able to access the explanations.

Over time, sharing these microlearnings within a school environment allows them to be accessed by other educators and students within the school and encourages a cross-curricular approach to STEAM education.

> I have only discovered the term "microlearnings" in the last two years but have realised that I have been using the concept for around 15 years. I used to teach students in a traditional classroom in a "teacher-led" format and find myself repeating the same instructions continually. While repetition is a key part of the teaching and learning environment, I started developing short videos and instructions for students to revisit when and if needed.
>
> These are ideal for those who need repetition and deserve differentiation. It also changed my educational approach from one that is teacher-focused to facilitator-focused. My students (and students from other classes) are aware of where skill-building microlearnings are available and seek them out on an as-needed basis.

CHAPTER 21

# A cross-curricular and extra-curricular approach

## Developing your cross-curricular approach

Once the basic structure has been introduced within some of the key teaching and learning areas, it is time to then extend to other areas. The design thinking and project-based learning skills developed as part of STEAM can be easily incorporated into other teaching and learning areas.

This is something that occurs more naturally in a primary school environment but is often lost within the silos of secondary education. One way to establish this approach is to look at mapped programs and develop tasks that incorporate science, technology, engineering, art and/or mathematics. This might be achieved via:

- Adding STEAM components to tasks built by other teaching areas, or
- Matching up units of work across teaching areas so that what is being taught in one area enhances what is being taught in another.

Some simple examples of how this might be done are given below.

- Talking about body image in health, and teaching Photoshop skills at the same time, with the theme "Is seeing believing?" Students gain understanding of how mainstream media enhance images to appear perfect, while in health they are taught about what helps define our body image, and how this affects our overall mental health and wellbeing.
- Using Microbits to capture data on the speed of an object. Microbits can be added to the top of an object, and they can capture data. This data can be added to Excel spreadsheets and manipulated into charts. The data can then be used in mathematics and/or science to analyse motion or speed. This would fit into statistics, digital technology, and laws of motion.

- Developing students' critical thinking processes in subjects such as history. The approach would be to break historical events into either:
  - Data-flow diagrams showing how the order of events led to certain outcomes
  - Mind maps to show the important components of a historical event.

  Students can then be challenged to identify either:
  - Critical points where events might have changed
  - Points where, if an outcome had been different (e.g. a failed assassination attempt or lost battle), the historical event might have taken a different path
  - What the past can tell us about future events and what their outcomes might be.

  Problem-solving and adjusting will help to develop students' critical and computational thinking.
- Using ChatGPT to enable students working within history to have AI "conversations" with historical leaders. Students are able to create questions for their chosen historical figures (e.g. Albert Einstein, Henry VIII) for research, such as: "Act as Henry VIII and answer the following questions about your time as king".
- Creating a showcase for students' artwork using ThingLink (or similar products) to create a virtual tour for your students' artwork or research into artists. ThingLink is a product that can use 360-degree cameras, videos or still images to create "rooms" and link to outside websites, puzzles and so on. It can be used in conjunction with VR headsets on a computer or tablet to improve viewing. (See ThingLink, page 177.)
- In PE it is possible to create short videos for equipment usage and add them to QR codes. Students can then see how to use equipment and ensure health and safety guidelines are met.

## Supporting staff across learning areas

The biggest issue in gaining traction with STEAM across the curriculum is lack of time and support. Support is needed to:

- Develop curriculum programs
- Update staff and student skills within areas of technology
- Make training available on an as-needed basis.

One key to this is the availability of training resources. In the same way that microlearnings are great for students, they can also be a wonderful support for educators. The storage of these learnings in appropriate categories and in an easily accessible space is vital. Ideally the microlearnings will be available for staff and students in an appropriate learning management system (LMS), and staff will be made aware that they are available for use at any time.

Targeted training for individual staff is also an effective approach. This can be in the form of in-house professional learning or focused assessment development. Another great way to improve staff team teaching and collaboration is for one educator to teach content and skills with another observing and supporting. As we know, the best way to learn something is to teach it to others, so this method has worked successfully in the past.

> At my school, a learning showcase approach is used to support professional development. Staff across the school are encouraged to showcase work and challenges that they are using within their programs. This is not completed in a formal "chalk and talk" way, but in a "browse, immerse, discuss, apply" format. Educators who have completed a task or learning experience or used a new piece of software or equipment are encouraged to showcase that in a practical way. Staff then "play" with the task and discuss what they like about it, why it worked well, and how they could include something similar in their own learning area.
>
> This has been very effective in improving staff collegiality and the advancement of new techniques and methodology. It is much more effective than being talked at in a lecture format.

## Girls in STEAM

There is a definite gender gap within digital technology and STEAM programs. In primary schools, the uptake of STEAM is higher for girls than it is in secondary schools. There are several reasons for this, but the overall challenge is to get girls back into STEAM and keep them there. The skills are too essential to future success to be only reaching half of a school community.

Much research has been focused on the disparity between male and female participation and where that disparity starts. For example, Master et al. (2017) found that "gender gaps begin early; young girls report less interest and self-efficacy in technology compared with boys in elementary school". They conclude that the "first step toward increasing women's individual interest in computer science and engineering is to trigger young girls' situational interest in topics such as robotics". The evidence, then, points towards the early implementation of STEAM programs in a supportive and engaging learning environment.

Many of the components that are key to the Authentic STEAM Framework are also the components that encourage girls to be part of a STEAM environment. These include:

- Creating situations and programs that involve mentors and topic experts. These do not always need to be female experts and mentors, but all students react well to seeing how people use STEAM in the real world. Marion Edelman's quote "You can't be what you can't see" is so true. Showing the ways in which people are building expertise and experience in STEAM fields is essential to inclusion.

  González-Pérez et al. (2020) discuss the importance of female role models in STEM education. Their research shows that "the role-model intervention has a positive and significant effect on mathematics enjoyment, importance attached to math, expectations of success in math, and girls' aspirations in STEM, and a negative effect on gender stereotypes. Additionally, the female role-model sessions significantly increase the positive impact of expectations of success on STEM choices".

- Focusing on creating STEAM challenges with links to real-world issues. This is something that makes learning more relevant. To engage students and particularly girls into STEAM, the most authentic tasks are the most successful. Instead of simplifying and limiting tasks, educators should "promote multiple cycles of design so that students create complex solutions and products, design powerful interdisciplinary projects" (Blikstein, 2013).

- Providing coding and challenges that focus on interests and information that appeal to girls. This is more about creating choices within coding and challenge environments and encouraging creativity.

Overall, the idea is to create situations and opportunities where girls (and effectively all students) can see where they fit in the world and how they can contribute to it.

## Extra-curricular programs

One way to enhance the introduction of STEAM outside the standard school environment is through the development of a lunchtime or after-school program in STEAM challenge learning. Extra-curricular STEAM programs are key to overall success in STEAM education, as they provide an essential component of the learning ecosystem. A learning ecosystem may be described as a system that focuses on the student at its centre and "works intentionally and collaboratively to create a rich educational world for children and youth as they grow into adults" (Krishnamurthi et al., 2014).

The importance of STEAM programs cannot be underestimated. Increasingly, "schools are seeking strategies that introduce STEAM concepts and reinforce classroom learning. Afterschool programs provide time for projects, self-guided exploration, and supplemental programming to build skills, confidence, and ongoing interest in STEAM" (Alton, 2022).

Extra-curricular STEAM programs have great importance because:

- They allow students who are keen on STEAM and not athletically-minded to be part of a team-building experience.
- They become visible to the whole school and can generate interest from many areas, which will in turn help to build the program.
- They enable students to develop their critical and computational skills in a positive and fun-filled environment.

To enable the success of extra-curricular STEAM programs, it is necessary to have a fully planned program rather than an ad hoc system. This is to ensure that there is a continued build-up of skills and expectations over time.

The benefits of quality after-school programs can be many and varied. Krishnamurthi et al. (2014) assert that "high-quality afterschool programs have found that participating children see a significant improvement in their self-perception, increased positive social behavior and a decrease in problem behaviors – changes that ultimately extend to school-related behavior. Hence, afterschool programs are increasingly seen as a key social and academic support for youth".

While creating an after-school program is a wonderful decision for your school, the type of program that is developed is important to ensure its success. As Alton (2022) states, the program should not be an "extension of classroom time; instead, look for ways to encourage students to follow their natural curiosity and interests".

Some of the ways that this might be achieved are:

- Participation in programs such as robotics and coding challenges

- Exposure to external mentors who can present varied skills to students – these could include environmental, engineering, aquaculture or chemistry experts
- Developing a "maker space" to allow exploration and innovation
- Open-ended challenges that allow for multiple outcomes
- Online events such as:
    - eSports challenges
    - Bebras computational thinking challenges (https://www.bebras.org)
    - Entrepreneurial challenges such as Enterprize's Spark Challenge (https://enterprize.space/programs/)
- Focusing on current events, including cybersecurity, cyberbullying and current digital technology issues.

## Maker spaces

A maker space is not essential to a successful STEAM program but is certainly something that will help to support your program as it develops. Maker spaces are separate areas or rooms that allow students to spark their imaginations and bring ideas to life. The creation of a maker space can build student agency and ownership of the space, and is a way to build the vision and evolution of STEAM within the school community.

While maker spaces can vary in design and evolution, some essential components of a maker space are:

- Good ventilation and light
- A safe environment for students to work in
- Large tables for working on tasks
- Stationery, pens and markers for design
- Whiteboards and pinboards for design and group work
- Basic tools such as pliers, glue guns, tape and scissors
- Lockable cupboards and the ability to restrict access to the room.

Items such as VR headsets, 3D printers, laser cutters and CNC routers would be wonderful, but the cost of providing these items may be prohibitive. However, it is still possible to create an engaging environment for learning without them.

The size, space and contents of a maker space are less important than the idea that they exist. Rendina (2017) argues that "Makerspaces come in all shapes and sizes, but they all serve as a gathering point for tools, projects, mentors and expertise. A collection of tools does not define a makerspace. Rather, we define it by what it enables: making". So, having a limited range of components is not a reason to delay beginning. Begin, then add items as time and finances allow. It is the meeting, gathering, discussion and experimentation that are essential.

# PART 7
# AUTHENTIC ASSESSMENTS

"All truths are easy to understand once they are discovered.
The point is to discover them."

– GALILEO GALILEI

CHAPTER 22

# Creating personalised contracts

Standard practice within education is for teachers to create assessments for students to complete. While this is still true, within STEAM and digital technology, creating personalised contracts with students aids in the development of student agency.

## Components

The key components of a strong contract-based system are:

- A consistent approach to contracting in which students know what to expect from the process
- An interactive approach to the development of the contract between the teacher (acting as facilitator) and student
- A realistic understanding of what can be produced within the timeframe of the contract
- Set deadlines and scaffolding in place to keep the student accountable, rather than one final end point
- If working in groups, the ability of students to assign roles and tasks, and keep track of who is doing what and in what order
- Regular meetings with the teacher to discuss progress and completion.

## Deliverables

Students and teachers alike need to have a clear idea of deliverables – in other words, what needs to be passed in. These should be included in the terms of the contract and referred back to in regular meetings.

A key deliverable when working with contracts and negotiations is the use of a written journal – either handwritten or in Word. This allows students to keep track of the iterative process that has led to a solution and the completion of the requirements of the contract. The amount of detail and the content will change with each contract.

Another key deliverable is the initial negotiated contract and the final reflection on the negotiated project. This is essential to effective completion of and reflection on the project. It would be expected that there would be some variation between what the student expected they could complete and what actually was completed.

This is an important part of building resilience and student agency. It allows students to begin to understand how well they can use their time and reflect on their management of that time. It will also help them to work on areas for improvement and deepen their ability to plan tasks effectively. It is essential that contract negotiation is student led – your role as a facilitator is to guide them to develop something that is achievable but will stretch them in their capabilities.

I occasionally have students who like to work in one area – e.g. Photoshop – and continue to do the same tasks again and again. My key input into these processes is to ask: "How is this helping you extend your learning?" I require them to go outside their comfort zone, even just a little bit.

Below are samples of the **Negotiated project proposal** and the **Final reflection for negotiated project**. These are stored in either printed or electronic form and referred back to throughout the timeframe of the contract.

# Negotiated project proposal

| | |
|---|---|
| Student name | |
| Student subject | |
| What is your proposed project? | |
| What software and resources will you use? | |
| What skills did you develop during this project? | |
| How do these skills relate back to the assessment rubric for your subject? | |
| Are there any links to tutorials that you have already identified for use? | |
| What support do you need from your facilitator? | |
| What will your deliverables be at the end of the project? | |
| Teacher's observations and guidance (to be filled in by your teacher) | |

# Final reflection for negotiated project

| Student name | |
| --- | --- |
| Student subject | |
| What was your proposed project? | |
| How do you feel you met the requirements you set out for yourself? | |
| What skills did you develop during this project? | |
| What challenges did you meet within the development of your project? | |
| What did you expect to be producing at the end of the project? | |
| How do your end products relate to what you set out initially? | |
| What did you do well within this project? | |
| What could you have done better? | |
| What can you change in order to make that happen? | |
| Teacher's observations and guidance (to be filled in by your teacher) | |

## CHAPTER 23

# The theory behind updating how we assess

There are many traditional assessment formats carried out in schools. This is one of the most regularly used formats:

1. Students are given information via a PowerPoint, video or other format.
2. They then complete some consolidation tasks that reinforce what they have learnt.
3. They may complete an assignment related to the task.
4. Finally, they complete an assessment in some form, often a written test, in which they are asked to regurgitate what they have learnt.
5. After this they move onto another topic, where the process begins all over again.

This is the way many have been taught in the past and many are still being taught. Teaching in essence has not changed since the days of blackboards and slates. Overhead projectors, smartboards, whiteboards, PowerPoint slides – none of these have essentially changed the way we teach. A major portion of our students' educational experience still involves sitting and listening, rather than thinking and doing.

Many of the artificial intelligence options that support educators in building PowerPoint slides, worksheets, tests and so on are wonderful time-savers. However, we are still focusing on creating assessments and tasks that do not focus on the real problem – developing pedagogy and learning to the point where students are long-term learners who are developing skills that will help them adapt to and engage with an ever-changing work environment.

In her TED Talk, Hardman (2023) discusses the need to optimise learning by creating a "system of instruction more about proposing problems, projects, learning not by being told something but by being asked something. Learning by exploration and research. Learning by getting things wrong then correcting them".

Hardman goes on to say that this approach of active learning has been shown to improve outcomes for *all* learners but particularly those disengaged or disadvantaged by traditional teaching and learning styles.

So how does this tie in with STEAM education? Through the development of real-life, challenge-based tasks, students can:

- Be engaged more effectively
- Learn essential problem-solving skills
- Be adaptable and courageous in their approach to learning
- Develop resilience in educational and life experiences.

This last point is essential. By seeing errors as a step towards further learning, and eliminating unproductive paths, it is possible to enhance learning in a positive way.

Below is an example from my own teaching experience that illustrates the importance of each of these steps. This framework has been developed over a long period of trial and error, and when I began examining the process for others to use, it was important to work out success criteria for the Authentic STEAM Framework.

**Grade 9 robotics class**

One of my students came to me and asked if he could join someone else's group, as his robot was not working properly. At that point I could have acquiesced or made some suggestions. Instead, something made me pause, and I waited to see what the other students would say. Their responses came in quick and fast:

- "But that's the whole point – if something doesn't work, you can eliminate that and then find another way."
- "Try and remember the point where things went wrong. Backtrack to there and find another path."
- "Just keep trying – you'll get there. Most of it is good. You just need to change a few things."

This sample of responses represents to me the holy grail of teaching: to "build" students over time who are able to say "Yes" to any challenge; to be confident that even though they do not know how to do something, they will be able to work it out and problem-solve to create a successful solution. I do not use the term "build" lightly or ironically. As an educator, I see that my role is to enable students to reach their full potential, while simultaneously empowering them with the tools to solve any problem. My teaching style is to be a facilitator, and my overarching aim is to make myself redundant in the process, as is shown in the above example.

This is represented well by Krauss and Prottsman (2017), who state that "when students learn that each failure is a clue for what they try next, they stop thinking of failure as a frustration, and begin to look at it as an element of exploration". That is where the success lies; that is where we look to become facilitators and mentors rather than the bringers of all knowledge.

Steuer (2023) also discusses the idea of failure as having a positive impact on the growth of students: "by modelling a healthy process for growth without requiring perfection, we teach our students growth mindset". "Growth mindset" is the ability of someone to continue to adapt and grow over time, developing resilience and believing in their own capability to shine.

If we are using STEAM to develop desired skills in students, we will need to adjust our assessment methods to fit this new style of teaching and learning. To be successful in assessing within a STEAM environment, it will be necessary to focus on the process and the development of skills, not just on an attempt at a final assessment task. This leads to the idea of performance-based assessment.

Performance-based assessment is an important aspect of the process of assessment within the STEAM environment. In Tasmania we use criterion-based assessment, which is the same process with a different name. Gyamfi et al. (2023) state that performance-based assessment is "characterised by assessing multiple learning targets, especially with tasks that require the students to create objects, produce a report, or put up a demonstration of an activity or event". Using performance-based assessment requires teachers to look beyond the tradition format of education and determine how well a student understands and applies knowledge.

McTighe & Ferrara (1998) describe three types of performance-based assessment – namely, product, performance and process-oriented assessments.

## Product

The product component of performance-based assessment relates to the result that is produced, based on the challenge or task set. This is always a tangible response, and could include (but is not restricted to):

- Video
- Prototype or model
- Poster
- Animation

- Interpretive dance (!)
- Laboratory report
- Essay or short written response.

## Process

The process component of performance-based assessment focuses on the design, thinking and problem-solving component of any task – for example:

- **Analysis** – the inquiry into what is required to complete the task
- **Research** – the information-gathering that has gone into the process of completing the task
- **Design** – the options for design and solution that have gone into the completion of the task
- **Development** – the building of the final solution of the task
- **Teamwork** – the interaction, task sharing and workload balance required to complete the task
- **Evaluation and testing** – the ability of the students to look at what they have completed and then evaluate whether it meets the needs of the task and what they might need to adjust. If required, this may be completed in tandem with the testing component. Testing allows students to review their responses and see if the solution works as required.

Ultimately, process and process-oriented assessment does not require a program or response to be fully completed. What it requires is that clear thought processes have gone into the completion of the task, and an iterative procedure has been thoroughly worked through to refine what is required within the task. The process is more important than the end point.

> When students begin working in this way within my classes, they often feel some stress around whether their program or solution is fully working at the end of the process. As time goes on, though, they realise that the completion of the task is less important than the process they use to get through to the end product. The key factor in the assessment of all of my tasks is to be able to see:
> - Growth of understanding through development and research
> - Good decision-making through testing and evaluation
> - Understanding of what has worked well and why
> - An iterative process that grows further towards an effective solution as time passes.
>
> Remember, the journey is more important than the destination.

To be able to assess these components, the following strategies are very useful:

- **Embracing drafts and multiple completion dates.** Students are required to share a folder containing all documentation and references. At specific points, the content is marked, and advice is given that supports reaching an appropriate end point.
- **Journals.** The journal is an essential component of this type of teaching and learning methodology. It allows the student and the educator to work through a process that shows what has been done, what the possible choices are, how decisions were made, and where the project could go to from here.
- **Documentation.** Documentation is also an essential component of this process-oriented approach. This can be presented in a template form with headings and requirements or given with dot points of what is required for the final assessment. The creation of user guides or instructional videos can also be a useful skill for students and educators alike to obtain. To be able to show understanding and depth of knowledge, explaining the process to another person can be beneficial. What is intuitive to one is not intuitive to all, and being able to adapt to that mindset is beneficial for all concerned.

  An important component to include in documentation is an evaluation of what went well, what would be changed if time allowed, and what would be nice additions to have. These insights are often very revealing in terms of building a clear view of the challenges faced and the victories won.
- **Peer- and self-evaluation.** Being able to show a realistic understanding of how to work within a team, and what the contribution of all team members was, is essential to process versus product assessment practices. This should be done regularly during the draft process, by both the students and the team as appropriate.
- **Rubrics.** Using assessment rubrics to assess tasks can be extremely useful and should be added to the task sheet when the assessment is passed out. This allows students to gain an understanding of how they will be assessed and what they can do at each stage to show their deeper understanding of the requirements for assessment.

There are several students I have worked with who are very proficient with software, and other than setting challenging tasks, need very little support in that area. In this situation, I see my role as a facilitator as one that requires me to support them in communicating and documenting their processes and outputs in such a way that they improve their inter-personal skills and understand what is needed from other points of view. Often this is a much harder process than teaching software requirements. But it has far-reaching effects. The main methods that I use for this type of educational development is the creation of user guides, instruction sets and instructional videos. In some cases, it is as simple as getting the student to explain the process to another student, rather than just doing it for them quickly without explaining what is happening.

Some of the assessment methods that work well with STEAM are peer- and self-assessment. I often use the same template for both types of assessment, as it allows me to quickly compare their own view of their assessment, and their view of what others have achieved within the process. Sample templates for each section are shown in the following pages.

# Authentic STEAM peer- and self-assessment (simplified)

| | |
|---|---|
| Challenge name<br>Student name<br>Group members<br>1<br>2<br>3<br>4 | How well did we research information?<br>1.<br>2.<br>3.<br>4. |
| How well did we design and create in our group?<br>1.<br>2.<br>3.<br>4. | How well did we present information?<br>1.<br>2.<br>3.<br>4. |
| What did we do well? | What could we do better |

# Authentic STEAM peer- and self-assessment (detailed)

| | | | | | | |
|---|---|---|---|---|---|---|
| **Student name** | | | | | | |
| **Challenge name** | | | | | | |
| **Group members** | | | | | | |
| **Stimulus and resources** | How well did each group member participate in:<br>• The understanding of the stimulus?<br>• The development of the resources? | | | | | |
| **Brainstorm and research** | How well did each group member participate in:<br>• The brainstorming of ideas?<br>• The research process? | | | | | |
| **Prototype and simulate** | How well did each group member participate in:<br>• The prototyping process?<br>• The refinement process? | | | | | |
| **Present and evaluate** | How well did each group member participate in:<br>• The presentation process?<br>• The evaluation process? | | | | | |

# Authentic STEAM rubric

This rubric is designed to be a basic starting point, and to be adjusted to the relevant criteria or requirements that are necessary for individual tasks. Three alternatives for column headings have been placed in the top row and may be adapted depending on what is suitable.

| Criteria | A<br>Exceptional<br>*Well above requirements* | B<br>Proficient<br>*Above requirements* | C<br>Basic<br>*At requirements* | D<br>Limited<br>*Below requirements* |
|---|---|---|---|---|
| **Stimulus and resources** | Demonstrates a deep understanding of the stimulus and contributes significantly to its interpretation. Proactively engages in developing high-quality resources. | Shows a good understanding of the stimulus and contributes effectively to resource development. Actively participates in resource creation. | Demonstrates a basic understanding of the stimulus. Contributes to resource development with some limitations. | Struggles to understand the stimulus. Contributes minimally to resource development. |
| **Brainstorm and research** | Actively participates in the brainstorming process, contributing innovative and insightful ideas. Plays a key role in the comprehensive research process. | Contributes well to the brainstorming process with creative ideas. Demonstrates effective participation in the research phase. | Participates in the brainstorming process with basic ideas. Shows some contribution to the research phase. | Offers minimal input during brainstorming. Contributes little to no research efforts. |

The theory behind updating how we assess

| Criteria | A<br>Exceptional<br>*Well above requirements* | B<br>Proficient<br>*Above requirements* | C<br>Basic<br>*At requirements* | D<br>Limited<br>*Below requirements* |
|---|---|---|---|---|
| Prototype and simulate | Takes a lead role in the design process, contributing innovative and well-thought-out ideas.<br>Actively engages in refining the prototype. | Contributes effectively to the design process with thoughtful ideas.<br>Participates actively in the refinement of the prototype. | Participates in the design process with basic ideas.<br>Shows some effort in refining the prototype. | Contributes minimally to the design process.<br>Limited involvement in refining the prototype. |
| Present and evaluate | Delivers a compelling and well-organised presentation.<br>Offers insightful contributions during the evaluation process. | Presents effectively, maintaining clarity and engagement.<br>Provides valuable input during the evaluation phase. | Presents with some organisation, but may lack clarity at times.<br>Offers basic input during the evaluation process. | Struggles to present ideas coherently.<br>Contributes minimally to the evaluation phase. |

# Conclusion

> "Learning starts with failure; the first failure is the beginning of education." – John Hersey

The conclusion to this book should not be seen as an ending, but as a beginning. My hope is that our conversation is just a starting point for you, and that you know you can come back again and again until you get where you need to go. Begin where you are, and just keep saying "Yes" to challenges that you face as an educator. It does get easier. Give your students the educational experiences that mould them to be excited about their learning.

Ultimately, our students all want to be seen, heard, understood and accepted. I hope that by changing how we educate our students, and how we build our learning experiences, who they are will come more to the forefront, so this can happen more easily and effectively.

Is this an idealistic thought? Probably.

But is it achievable? Absolutely. Our students are worth the additional effort.

The benefits of STEAM education are unlimited, particularly when planned and presented in a thoughtful, strategic and enjoyable way. The aim is to produce resilient, creative and innovative students, who are taught by enthusiastic, well-prepared educators – to create an environment where every student reaches their potential.

Finally, it is at the core of who I am as an educator to believe that who we are, and how we conduct ourselves, makes a difference to who they are. Writing this book has reignited the spark of all that I hold dear about education and has shown me that I still have more to give. What we do is important and far-reaching – let's make that gift a positive one.

Thank you for the chat – let's keep talking!

*Michelle*
STEAMauthenticity.com

# Bibliography

Allison, M., & Kendrick, L. M. (2015). Toward education 3.0: Pedagogical affordances and implications of social software and the semantic web. *New Directions for Teaching and Learning, 2015*(144), 109–119. https://doi.org/10.1002/tl.20167

Almulla, M. A. (2020). The effectiveness of the project-based learning (PBL) approach as a way to engage students in learning. *SAGE Open, 10*(3). https://doi.org/10.1177/2158244020938702

Alton, L. (2022). *Could an afterschool program be your STEAM curriculum's secret weapon?* Connected. https://community.connection.com/could-an-afterschool-program-be-your-steam-curriculums-secret-weapon/

Ananda, L., Rahmawati, Y., & Khairi, F. (2023). Critical thinking skills of chemistry students by integrating design thinking with STEAM-PjBL. *Journal of Technology and Science Education, 13*(1), 352–67. http://dx.doi.org/10.3926/jotse.1938

Baber, H. (2021). Social interaction and effectiveness of the online learning: A moderating role of maintaining social distance during the pandemic COVID-19. *Asian Education and Development Studies, 11*(1):159–71. https://doi.org/10.1108/AEDS-09-2020-0209

Bertolini, A. (2022). *Igniting STEM learning: A guide to designing an authentic primary school STEM program.* Hawker Brownlow Education.

Blikstein, P. (2013). Digital fabrication and "making" in education: The democratization of invention, *FabLabs: Of Machines, Makers and Inventors, 4*(1), 1–21.

Dutta, A., & Rangnekar, S. (2022). Preference for teamwork, personal interaction and communities of practice: Does co-worker support matter? *VINE Journal of Information and Knowledge Management Systems.* https://doi.org/10.1108/vjikms-11-2021-0284

Gajderowicz, T., Jakubowski, M., Wrona, S., & Alkhadim, G. (2023). Is students' teamwork a dreamwork? A new DCE-based multidimensional approach to preferences towards group work. *Humanities and Social Sciences Communications, 10*(1). https://doi.org/10.1057/s41599-023-01641-x

Ghafar, Z., & Abdullkarim, S. (2023). Microlearning as a learning tool for teaching and learning in acquiring language: Applications, advantages, and influences on the language. *Canadian Journal of Educational and Social Studies, 3*(2), 45–62. https://doi.org/10.53103/cjess.v3i2.127

González-Pérez, S., Mateos de Cabo, R., & Sáinz, M. (2020). Girls in STEM: Is it a female role-model thing? *Frontiers in Psychology, 11.* https://doi.org/10.3389/fpsyg.2020.02204

Green, O. (2021). *Think unique: Your comprehensive guide to cultivating tomorrow's innovators through project-based learning.* Glittering Minds Pty Ltd.

Gyamfi, A., Langee, P., Yeboah, A., & Adu, I. A. (2023). Performance-based assessment in contemporary classroom assessment: The forms and nature. *Asian Research Journal of Arts & Social Sciences, 19*(4), 1–7. https://doi.org/10.9734/arjass/2023/v19i4431

Hardman, P. (2023). The AI education revolution is coming – or is it? *TED Talk*. https://www.ted.com/talks/dr_philippa_hardman_the_ai_education_revolution_is_coming_or_is_it (accessed 2 October 2023).

Heard, J., Scoular, C., Duckworth, D., Ramalingam, D., & Teo, I. (2020). Critical thinking: Skill development framework. Australian Council for Educational Research. https://research.acer.edu.au/ar_misc/4

Henriksen, D. (2017). Creating STEAM with design thinking: Beyond STEM and arts integration. *STEAM*, *3*(1), 1–11. https://doi.org/10.5642/steam.20170301.11

Hölzle, K., & Rhinow, H. (2019). The dilemmas of design thinking in innovation projects. *Project Management Journal*, *50*(4), 418–30. https://doi.org/10.1177/8756972819853129

ISTE. (2021). We are ISTE. https://cdn.iste.org/ (accessed 2 August 2023).

Krauss, J., & Prottsman, K. (2017). *Computational thinking and coding for every student: The teacher's getting-started guide*. Corwin, SAGE Publishing Company.

Krishnamurthi, A., Ballard, M., & Noam, G. G. (2014). *Examining the impact of afterschool STEM programs*. Distributed by ERIC Clearinghouse.

Lal, R., & Lal, M. (2011). Web 3.0 in education & research. *BVICAM's International Journal of Information Technology*, *3*(2), 335–40.

Lee, D. (2018). *Design thinking in the classroom: Easy-to-use teaching tools to foster creativity, encourage innovation and unleash potential in every student*. Ulysses Press.

Li, J., Luo, H., Zhao, L., Zhu, M., Ma, L., & Liao, X. (2022). Promoting STEAM education in primary school through cooperative teaching: A design-based research study. *Sustainability*, *14*(16), 10333. http://dx.doi.org/10.3390/su141610333

Martinez, S., and Prensky, M., 2021. Point/counterpoint: Is the digital native a myth? *Learning & Leading with Technology*, *39*(3), 6. https://www.iste.org/node/6569 (accessed 1 August 2023).

Master, A., Cheryan, S., Moscatelli, A., & Meltzoff, A. N. (2017). Programming experience promotes higher stem motivation among first-grade girls. *Journal of Experimental Child Psychology*, *160*, 92–106. https://doi.org/10.1016/j.jecp.2017.03.013

McTighe, J., & Ferrara, S. (1998). *Assessing learning in the classroom*. Washington, DC: National Education Association.

Nazdan, S. (2018). Flipped learning 2.0: Rethinking the flipped classroom model. *Getting Smart*. https://www.gettingsmart.com/2018/07/28/flipped-learning-2-0-rethinking-the-flipped-classroom-model/

*OECD Future of Education and Skills 2030*. https://www.oecd.org/education/2030-project/

PBL Toolkit. (2023). https://pbltoolkit.weebly.com/

Rendina, D. (2017). *Defining makerspaces: What the research says*. Renovated Learning. http://www.renovatedlearning.com/2015/04/02/defining-makerspaces-part-1/

Robinson, K. (2006). Do schools kill creativity? *TED Talk*. https://www.ted.com/talks/sir_ken_robinson_do_schools_kill_creativity (accessed 2 October 2023).

Schwartz, D. L., Tsang, J. M., & Blair, K. P. (2016). *The ABCs of how we learn: 26 scientifically proven approaches, how they work, and when to use them*. New York: W.W. Norton.

Sinek, S. (2009). How great leaders inspire action. *TED Talk*. https://www.ted.com/talks/simon_sinek_how_great_leaders_inspire_action?language=en (accessed 8 November 2023).

Stehle, S. M., & Peters-Burton, E. E. (2019). Developing student 21st century skills in selected exemplary inclusive STEM high schools. *International Journal of STEM Education*, *6*(1). https://doi.org/10.1186/s40594-019-0192-1

Steuer, R. (2023). *PBL simplified: 6 steps to move project-based learning from idea to reality*. Morgan James Publishing.

Susilana, R., Dewi, L., Rullyana, G., Hadiapurwa, A., & Khaerunnisa, N. (2022). Can microlearning strategy assist students' online learning? *Jurnal Cakrawala Pendidikan, 41*(2). https://doi.org/10.21831/cp.v41i2.43387

Tofade, T., Elsner, J., & Haines, S. T. (2013). Best practice strategies for effective use of questions as a teaching tool. *American Journal of Pharmaceutical Education, 77*(7), 155. https://doi.org/10.5688/ajpe777155

Voicu, C., Ampartzaki, M., Yilmaz Dogan, Z., & Kalogiannakis, M. (2023). STEAM implementation in preschool and primary school education: Experiences from six countries. In M. Ampartzaki and M. Kalogiannakis (Eds.) *Early childhood education: Innovative pedagogical approaches in the post-modern era*. IntechOpen. https://doi.org/10.5772/intechopen.107886

Walsh, K., & Elmslie, L. (2005). Practicum pairs: An alternative for first field experience in early childhood teacher education. *Asia-Pacific Journal of Teacher Education, 33*(1), 5-21.

www.ingramcontent.com/pod-product-compliance
Lightning Source LLC
Chambersburg PA
CBHW071307110526
44591CB00010B/813